UNDERSTANDING INTELLIGENCE

Ken Richardson

OPEN UNIVERSITY PRESS

Milton Keynes · Philadelphia

Open University Press
Celtic Court
22 Ballmoor
Buckingham
MK18 1WX

and
1900 Frost Road, Suite 101
Bristol, PA 19007, USA

First Published 1991

British Library Cataloguing in Publication Data

Richardson, Ken
  Understanding intelligence.
  1. Man. Intelligence
  I. Title
  153.9
  ISBN 0–335–09398–1
  ISBN 0–335–09397–3 (pbk)

Library of Congress Cataloging-in-Publication Data

Richardson, Ken.
  Understanding intelligence/by Ken Richardson.
    p.   cm.
  Includes index.
  ISBN 0–335–09398–1 ISBN 0–335–09397–3 (pbk.)
  1. Intellect. I. Title
BF431.R415 1990
153.9-dc20   90–38874
                                              CIP

Typeset by Inforum Typesetting, Portsmouth
Printed in Great Britain by Biddles Limited, Guildford and Kings Lynn

Contents

Preface

The usual offering to psychology students on the subject of intelligence has rarely seemed satisfactory to me. A bit of the history of IQ will usually be included, followed by some review of the pros and cons of 'the test'. A brief review of the diverse 'structures' of intelligence proposed by a few famous names will often follow; and some account of the nature–nurture debate will usually be given, probably concluding with some safe 'middle-ground' position. More recently, a little about other 'approaches', such as the information-processing approach, or the developmental approach, has often been included in courses. And other special aspects may be thrown in, such as 'biological' aspects or something to do with the brain and intelligence. Sometimes the diversity and conflict that soon hits the student's own frontal lobes is rationalised in terms of the value of an 'eclectic approach' to the understanding of intelligence.

What worries me, in sum, is that in the midst of these 'bits and pieces' students don't have a serious chance to get to grips with the real issues, and are left with a very fragmented impression and a few clichés. The problem is compounded, it seems to me, by the fact that so many books on intelligence are written by specialists who are promoting a particular 'line' offering perspectives rather uncritically, often with daunting technical language. On the other hand, there are many good critiques of 'IQ', but these are probably read only by a minority of students on an optional basis; and they may or may not attend to many of the more recent issues arising in the 'new' cognitive and developmental approaches to intelligence.

Meanwhile there seems little doubt that, for a variety of reasons, intelligence as a topic should continue to command the attention of psychologists and psychology students. Although more commonly avoided altogether in some psychology courses than it used to be, the 'idea' of intelligence (as a factor to be measured and controlled in experiments, say, or as a useful 'output' variable for assessing treatments of various kinds) is still pervasive; IQ testing is probably more prevalant than it has ever been; and we are constantly being told of 'new' ideas and approaches in intelligence, usually with the implication that these are free from the defects of the old. In addition, of course, there seems little doubt that what is made of test scores or other assessments of intelligence seriously affects people's lives, and that such effects are very widespread indeed.

The purpose of this book, then, is to help students obtain a critical purchase on the issues surrounding intelligence as a topic in psychology. This is done through the usual device of examining assumptions or preconceptions underlying common statements and theories of intelligence; examining how these in turn arise out of different social contexts in which different ideas about intelligence wax and wane; and of contrasting popular or informal conceptions with the demands of rigorous scientific theory. In addition, some broader perspectives are brought to bear on the subject than would ordinarily be the case. It is hoped that the result will provide a framework that will, in turn, help students organise their thoughts in a more critical, and therefore more productive, manner.

As usual in a work of this kind there is need to be selective, and some compromise between breadth and depth is inevitable. I hope this compromise has not done serious damage to the final result. Perhaps one of the most exciting aspects of human intelligence is the way that ideas are seldom, if ever, hatched in isolation from human history and the refracted thoughts of countless other people. I am grateful to my colleagues in the Centre for Human Development and Learning at the Open University for many comments and criticisms in the past, which I hope have resulted in some improvement in presentation, although I know that not all of them would agree with everything that is said here. Preoccupation with a work of this kind may well have led to a degree of neglect of other duties, and I hope I am forgiven for this. I am also grateful to many other individuals and groups in the past, too numerous to name here, whose thoughts are reflected in these pages, although responsibility for their particular expression is, of course, my own.

1

Intelligence in a word: popular and scientific conceptions

Introduction

Intelligence n. ability to understand, reason, and perceive, quickness in learning, mental alertness; ability to grasp relationships; information, news, *esp* military . . .

(Penguin Engish Dictionary 1964)

Intelligence. Wisdom – N. thinking power, intellectualism, intellect; brains, grey-matter, head, head-piece; nous, wit, commonsense; lights, understanding, sense, good s., horse s., gumption; wits, quick-thinking, readiness, esprit; capacity, calibre, IQ; forwardness, brightness; cleverness, brilliance, talent, genius . . .

(Roget's Thesaurus 1966)

Whether you prefer wit, horse sense or just plain common sense, intelligence is obviously a flexible concept with many meanings. By universal acknowledgement among psychologists, it is also one of the most elusive and slippery of ideas. At a popular level, intelligence seems to be readily recognised, because we use the word so liberally. Yet systematic observations have abundantly confirmed that we attribute people with intelligence on the basis of a wide diversity of signals or criteria: apparent 'cleverness', of course; but also self-presentation, speech and even facial appearance. Moreover, the term frequently becomes a convenient expression of our evaluations in a wide variety of domains, with a wide variety of subjects: I have just read a music reviewer, for example, describing a singer as having an 'intelligent voice'; in the same newspaper, I happened to notice a hot tip being described as an 'intelligent horse'.

Most people using the term as a convenient label aren't usually too bothered about precision in meaning. Grounded, probably, in little more than an intuition abstracted from everyday experience, the term helps us to communicate about the diversity we see among people. Such abstractions – we may call them concepts, or even informal theories – are very common indeed in helping us to make the enormous variety and uncertainty in the world we experience a little more predictable. Similar fuzzy terms and concepts are those of 'good/bad', 'noble/ignoble', and other 'dispositional traits', as philosophers call them.

Just because we have a name for something does not mean that the term has a clear referent; nor does it mean that it corresponds with anything actually existing. Our conceptual furniture consists of many idealistic 'unicorns'. Concepts of the flat earth, or the geocentric universe, or recourse to some inner essence or spirit agent, like phlogiston causing combustion or 'bad blood' causing disease, come into this category, all at one time having seemed so 'obvious' to observers both casual and careful. In spite of centuries of scientific advance many of our common concepts of the material world remain idealistic in this sense.

For example, investigators studying people's conceptions of the causes of the movement of objects, such as predicting the trajectories of objects dropped from aircraft, or in describing the 'forces' acting on objects thrown into the air, note adherence to a 'naive impetus' concept: i.e. a concept of a force imparted to the object at the start of its motion, and somehow petering out in the course of that motion, but which doesn't really exist. Similar naive conceptions about nature are found in a variety of other domains, too, such as electricity, heat and temperature, the nature of matter, and so on (see Driver *et al.* 1985). As Driver *et al.* note, such naive or popular conceptions appear to be idiosyncratic, lacking in coherence, and remarkably resistant to instruction or other counter-vailing evidence. The contrast, of course, is with ideal scientific concepts which are shared, coherent and open to modification.

What kind of concept is intelligence? It is the task of scholars (philosophers/scientists), of course, to clarify this murky conceptual furniture of everyday discourse, and provide us with a more reliable, detached and substantiated concept. And, once started, there is no knowing in advance where this process will end. In the course of their deliberations scholars may simply 'firm-up' the popular conception, perhaps with some modification; or they may (as with impetus) debunk it altogether, and produce some new constructions of their own, perhaps on the basis of some further observations.

Either way, the task is not an easy one. One reason for this is that the starting-point for any scholar considering ideas like intelligence is the same as that of the ordinary citizen, namely the uncertain variety of ordinary social experience. This difficulty is illustrated in Figure 1.1. Moreover, such scholars frequently have particular purposes and priorities in conducting their enquiries, and the answers they produce are bound to be related to the questions they ask. The first part of this chapter illustrates some of the meanderings of scholars, from antiquity to modern times, in trying to come to grips, for various purposes, with the concept of intelligence.

But empirical science is supposed to provide more reliable methods for

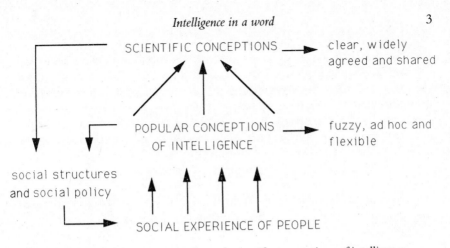

SCIENTIFIC CONCEPTIONS ⟶ clear, widely agreed and shared

POPULAR CONCEPTIONS OF INTELLIGENCE ⟶ fuzzy, ad hoc and flexible

social structures and social policy

SOCIAL EXPERIENCE OF PEOPLE

Figure 1.1   Relations between popular and scientific conceptions of intelligence

reaching the status of objective and detached theory, and these methods have been vigorously applied in the area of intelligence. Have psychologists, then, provided us with a *scientific* theory of intelligence? Few psychologists would argue that intelligence is a mature and coherent scientific concept, although it is investigated by scientists, written about in scientific journals, and so on. The reason for this may, again, be the very 'embeddedness' of the concept in social purpose and priorities. Scientists, too, live in a particular society; probably get paid to do a certain job within it; have their own social group or class affili-ations, and so on.

Not surprisingly, perhaps, surveys have shown a close correspondence be-tween 'scientific' and 'popular' notions of intelligence (e.g. Sternberg *et al.* 1981; Fry 1984). At the same time arguments rage about whether it is one thing or many; experts describe it in quite contradictory terms; psychologists are frequently proclaiming the construction of 'new ideas in intelligence' (An-derson 1989); but diverse conceptions remain remarkably resistant to modifica-tion. Method alone, then, does not free us from the preconceptions that even scientists must start with: included in the method must be the constant social criticism from which scientific consensus is ultimately wrought.

None the less, since most of contemporary investigation by psychologists in the domain of intelligence claims to be 'scientific', the second part of this chapter offers a very brief description of the aims and procedures of scientific investigation. This ought to provide a useful background to our subsequent appraisal of past and current scientific effort. Most of the rest of this book is, in fact, about the efforts of scientists to reach that much vaunted position of detached theory of intelligence. It illustrates the diversity of constructions that have emerged, and it offers criticism of these by identifying and assessing preconceptions and assumptions, and thus assessing the critical gap between an informal and a formal scientific theory as shown in Figure 1.1. The final chapter will offer some review and summary.

The general purpose of this first chapter is to obtain some impression of scholarly speculation prior to the modern, 'scientific' era. This is partly to show some of the diversity of formulation, and to consider how and why these formulations have changed from time to time. But such consideration is also instrumental in bringing us to consider how scientists today aim to replace the diktats of former ages with the disciplined procedures of scientific research and theory-building. So, after a brief historical overview of psychological ideas concerning intelligence, we turn, in the second part of the chapter, to consider how ideas generally are managed in science. As just mentioned, this should serve as useful background to the evaluation of the various 'modern' formulations and theories that are described in the rest of the book.

Intelligence in antiquity

A great many ideas in modern psychology stem from Ancient Greece, and this is particularly true of ideas about intelligence. For a long time, even then, philosopher-psychologists had been attempting to define and describe the human soul, and arrived at the tripartite division – the intellectual, the emotional and the appetitive – that is prevalent to this day (see Robinson 1981). But there were widely different views about the nature of this 'intellect' even then. The writings we know most about today, and to which modern ideas seem to be most obviously related, are those of Plato and Aristotle, produced around the third century BC.

Plato, the senior of the two, was writing in a curious period in the history of Athens; a time of political reaction to a long liberal period which had culminated in a series of disastrous military defeats. A new authoritarianism now held sway in a regime in which people were expected to know their place (Robinson 1981). Plato marshalled all his own intellectual resources in support of the regime. He wrote in support of rigid class divisions, claiming that they simply mirrored differences in innate intellectual strength among the populace. And in his *Republic* he wrote of the prerequisites of the perfect State, the structure of which would exactly reflect the intellectual attributes of its citizens.

In a way which is found in many informal, and some scientific, conceptions today, Plato was answering questions about *ranks* or *quantities* of intelligence, and how these qualified people for certain roles in society. He assumed that intellectual superiority marked the Rulers of his ideal state and was inborn. To improve the lot of the species he advocated a system of eugenic reproduction – marriage and reproduction confined to the Guardians (the Rulers). Using as an analogy the inequalities of metals, from gold to iron, he urged a vigilance about the 'characters' of people which, in terms of superstitious fear, finds many an echo in accounts of intelligence in the twentieth century:

> Therefore the first and most important of God's commandments to the
> Rulers is that they must excise their function as Guardians with

particular care in watching the mixture of metals in the characters of the children. If one of their own children has bronze or iron in its make-up, they must harden their hearts, and degrade it to the ranks of the industrial and agricultural class where it properly belongs. . . . For they know that there is a prophecy that the State will be ruined when it has Guardians of silver or bronze.

(Republic Book III)

But Plato had little to offer by way of further characterisation of this important entity. The intellect was obviously connected with a faculty of thought or conception – in particular, a power to apprehend relations and make abstractions (concepts, principles, rules, etc.). But above all he reasoned that it must be a *practical* power, because it was needed for the running of the State, for governing, planning, making decisions, and so on. Thus the good State was seen as a natural expression of the intelligence of its citizens, with a natural and convenient division of rank and duty according to inborn strength.

By the time of Aristotle, a generation later, the political pendulum had swung back the other way, and a much more liberal regime was in control. Quite different questions seem to have presented themselves to Aristotle, compared with those given priority by Plato. Accordingly he seems to have come up with some different answers. He attempted to characterise intelligence less in terms of social policy, and more in terms of its evolution among living things generally. Thus he saw intelligence as a common property of citizens (i.e. excluding slaves); the culmination of a system of 'psychic layers': 'that whereby the mind thinks and reasons'; and present only in humans. And he argued that 'intellectual virtue in the main owes its birth and its growth to teaching (for which reason it requires experience and time)'.

The Romans borrowed from and revised the Greek doctrines to suit their own view of the world. But it is from this period (largely in the writings of Cicero) that the modern term is thought to originate: strictly a compound, *intus lego*, meaning 'to read within me' or to read mentally, i.e. understanding. But the polarity of view about intelligence, the one a concept of a socially important 'strength' or 'power' on whose natural gradations (with vigilance) the survival of the state is hinged, the other a common characteristic of humans, and the object of detached study and characterisation, has persisted across the centuries, and forms the theme of the account which follows in this book.

The Middle Ages

Throughout the Middle Ages, with the rise of feudalism and the strength of the Church, the main virtue was for people to know their place – to be obedient to established authority – and this was reflected in the writings of scholars (themselves usually clerics). As a result, the idea of intelligence was tied up with ethical, political and social questions; the questions raised pervaded the institutions including, eventually, education.

In reaction to the upsurge in scholarship in the eighth to tenth centuries, learning itself was brought under institutional control. So Charlemagne decreed that education, hitherto private and haphazard, should be the concern of established schools throughout Europe, under the watchful eye of the Church. 'In every Bishop's See, and in every monastery, instruction shall be given in the psalms, musical notation, chant, the computation of years and seasons, and in grammar' (quoted in Hyman and Walsh 1973: 12). Response to such instruction thus soon became an important criterion of intelligence. As St Augustine wrote, 'the more acutely a boy understands . . . the more praiseworthy is he in point of ability' (quoted in Hyman and Walsh 1973). Response to schooling, and the distinction between 'bright' and 'dull' pupils, was thus already being made the 'test' of intelligence over a thousand years ago.

Over the next three or four centuries speculation began to grow about the forms and functions of intelligence. Attempts to characterise intelligence led to a variety of formulations. One account postulated a hierarchy of separate 'intelligences', each level proceeding or emanating from the other. Another distinguished the 'passive' (or sensory) intelligence from the 'active' (or cognitive) intelligence. Yet another distinguished the 'potential' from the 'acquired' intelligence. This particular distinction was held to explain how individuals may be widely different in their (acquired) understanding, while having the same potential. Duns Scotus identified a cognitive ability with two processes, the one 'intuitive', used in apprehending immediate reality (like recognising the black shapes on this paper as words); the other 'abstractive' (used in working out what the words mean). William of Ockham took up this distinction by claiming that the intuitive intelligence was 'in the senses', whereas abstractive intelligence goes beyond the here and now. Many attempts to characterise intelligence in the twentieth century seem to echo these early formulations, as we shall see.

Intelligence and equality

By the sixteenth century social, economic and ideological changes were taking place all over Europe. Over the next two hundred years the demand everywhere was for freedom (from feudal bonds) and equality (against the unequal power of the nobility). Correspondingly in the minds and writings of philosopher-psychologists, new emphases can be found in regard to individual intellectual differences. We need only consider the views of the two foremost scholars of the time, René Descartes and John Locke (who disagreed on much else), to appreciate this.

Descartes opened his *Discourse on Method* (published 1637) with the insistence that intellectual differences are ones of method and practice, rather than the expression of some natural variety:

Good sense is of all things in the world the most equally distributed . . . the power of forming a good judgement and of distinguishing the true from the false, which is properly speaking what is called good sense or reason, is by nature equal in all men. Hence . . . the diversity of our opinions does not proceed from some men being more rational than others, but solely from the fact that our thoughts pass through diverse channels and the same objects are not considered by all. For to be possessed of good mental powers is not sufficient; the principal matter is to apply them well.

(Haldane and Ross 1931)

And John Locke, who considered at great length the possibility of innate differences in mental strength, none the less reckoned that,

As it is in the body so it is in the mind; practice makes it what it is, and most even of those excellencies, which are looked on as natural endow- ments, will be found when examined into most narrowly, to be the product of exercise. . . . [Because] defects and weaknesses in men's un- derstanding, as well as other faculties, comes from a want of a right use of their own minds, I am apt to think that the fault is generally mislaid upon nature, and there is often a complaint of want of parts, when the fault lies in want of dire improvement of them.

(from *An Essay Concerning Human Understanding* 1690)

Intelligence and inequality

The relation between scholarly views of intelligence and economic inequalities and aspirations continued after the revolutions of the seventeenth and eight- eenth centuries. With the eclipse of the nobility and the rise of the new manufacturing class, new economic inequalities emerged. The rise of the manufacturing system at home brought degrees of exploitation and oppression that would have scandalised previous generations, while overseas, the search for raw materials and markets entailed the subjugation of other societies and the institutionalisation of slavery.

This brings us to the modern period, which has its roots firmly in the nineteenth century, and in particular in the writings of Herbert Spencer.

Herbert Spencer on intelligence

In his book *Principles of Psychology* (1855) Spencer devoted considerable time and space to the subject of intelligence, including three chapters entitled 'The Nature of Intelligence', 'The Law of Intelligence' and 'The Growth of Intelligence'. The result was a remarkable synthesis which had a profound impact on generations of psychologists. Indeed the framework constructed by Spencer, and the questions it was intended to answer, can still be found in modern ideas, so it is worth looking at them a little more closely.

To start with Spencer tried to characterise intelligence by relating it both to organic functions of living things generally, and to the evolution of living things, from organic life to psychic life. This therefore introduced a new dimension to previous *psycho*-logical characterisations, namely a *bio*-logical one, although Spencer interpreted the latter in terms of a rather mechanistic idea of adaptation:

> the fundamental condition of vitality is, that the internal state shall be continually adjusted to the external order. . . . If the relation of the internal order to the external order is one of but partial adjustment; the adaptation of inner to outer actions is imperfect; and life is proportionately low and brief. If between the inner and outer order the adjustment is complete; the adaptation is complete and the life is proportionately high and prolonged.
>
> (Spencer 1855: 506–7)

Determining the mechanism of this adaptation 'in the mind', was, to Spencer, the prime business of psychology. His own attempt to characterise it, however, led him to see it as a form of learning by association. This was an ancient idea, again stemming from Ancient Greece, that had become popular throughout the eighteenth and nineteenth centuries (see Richardson 1988). To Spencer, successful adaptation occurs when two or more objects or events associated in nature are also associated in their mental representations; that is when 'the persistency of the connection between two states of consciousness, is proportionate to the persistency of the connection between the phenomena to which they answer'. This correspondence principle is what Spencer called the Law of Intelligence.

But the correspondence can be of various grades. And Spencer distinguished three levels of correspondence: first, the *accuracy* of correspondence; second, the *number of cases* for which correspondence occurs; third, the *complexity of representation* 'answering to complexities in the environment'. These levels of intelligence are present in different degrees in different individuals, largely because they are transmitted from parents to offspring as if they were simple physical characteristics. As Spencer put it, 'mental peculiarities produced by habit become hereditary'.

This is a genetic theory known as 'the inheritance of acquired characteristics' that was eventually to be discredited. But the basic idea explained, to Spencer, and to those who followed him, the differences between nations and 'races', and between classes and individuals within nations. Thus although representations arise from experience, some people have the advantage of being born with 'pre-established relations'. Indeed 'the gradually-increasing intelligence displayed throughout childhood and youth, is in a much greater degree due to the completion of the cerebral organisation, than to the individual experience'

(1855: 582), and so 'it happens that faculties . . . which scarcely exist in the inferior human races, become congenital in the superior ones'.

The political and ideological advantages of Spencer's theory were immediately apparent. It apeared to give an acceptable justification of the miseries wreaked by the development of capitalism in the nineteenth century. It justified colonial exploitation and slavery. It was a corollary of Spencer's theory that 'the minds of the inferior human races cannot respond to relations of even moderate complexity . . . they can readily receive simple relations but not complex ones' (1855: 464). And it was a corollary of the same principle that the poor should not be allowed the benefit of social welfare and normal reproduction; as the 'unfit' they should simply be allowed to 'die off'.

Authority, reason and science

Intelligence, then, is not a subject only of the twentieth century. It has been the subject of great attention, and of an astonishing variety of formulation, since antiquity. Up to the nineteenth century there had been many attempts to characterise intelligence, some of the ingredients of which include

1 some kind of mental strength or power
2 the ability to abstract
3 to think or reason
4 to apprehend relations
5 good sense or judgement
6 to form complex (as opposed to simple) associations.

And of course it was perceived to vary in humans in consequence of

1 heredity (e.g. Plato; Spencer)
2 experience (e.g. Aristotle; Locke)
3 qualitative differences that cannot be quantified (or the use of different 'channels', as Descartes put it).

Finally, responsiveness to schooling long ago became the public 'test' of intelligence.

All of the ideas discussed so far were produced intuitively by people who, as it were, sucked them out of the end of a pencil; their persuasiveness to other people depended on the power and respectfulness of the authority stating them, or on their apparent consistency and reasonableness. The dilemma, of course, is that of knowing which of these are sound, and which are not; which are fact, and which are opinion or diktat. Here, in the criteria of knowledge, at least, there has been real advance.

Progress in the history of psychology, as in the history of ideas generally, is marked by two great achievements. First the passage from Authority to Reason: the shedding of 'truth by decree', or by authority, which pervaded so much of the Middle Ages, and the triumph of criticism, which stipulated argument, logic and consistency. The second triumph was the rise of science, and the dictum that the acceptability of propositions should be guided by certain rules of evidence and probability. Above all, the study of intelligence in the twentieth century has aimed to be *scientific*. The rest of this book is about the various works done around intelligence in the name of science. But in order to assess and evaluate these we need to remind ourselves what these rules are. This is what we shall now consider.

Theory: popular and scientific

Informal or popular theory

First of all we must try to demystify these daunting words 'theory' and 'science', and understand how 'scientific theory' is different from the way in which we normally represent and handle the world we live in. Both our scientific ways and our ordinary ways of living in the world, in fact, rely on abstraction, or generalisation from limited experience. This has already been indicated in Figure 1.1. Because the world we live in is one of constant novelty and change we cannot handle it by keeping a mental 'file' of familiar problems together with their pre-programmed solutions. For instance, you can drive your car down an unfamiliar road and deal with the unique problems presented by terrain and other traffic without a precise set of 'instructions' being available in advance. You can join a conversation at a party even though every sentence you hear is likely to be quite unique, in the sense that it is probably one that you have never heard before; as will be every sentence that you yourself utter. This coping with variability is partly true for all complex animals. But humans have a wholly new and even more complex layer of variability added to this in the form of a social-co-operative life-style that is seen in no other species.

Dealing with this change and variety is what intelligence is all about. We cannot deal with it through a system of reflexes. The latter would only be useful for fairly constant tasks in a fairly constant world. What means do we then use?

Probably the most popular current view is that we deal with the world by forming a mental model of it in some way. This idea has been around for a very long time (for example Craik 1943; see also Johnson-Laird 1983; Gentner and Stevens 1983). There is much debate about how such models are formed, and of their precise 'internal' structure. But they appear to act as informal theories of the world (see Murphy and Medin 1985).

Thus we each have informal theories about things like the weather, the workings of a car engine, human nature, the origins of children's personalities and, of course, intelligence. They emerge as abstractions in the course of our ordinary experience in these domains. They are important to us because first, they predict what might happen if we do this or that, or what will result if something else happens (e.g. if we impose sanctions on a child for bad behaviour, or the wind turns to the north); and second, we can trace the cause of something that *has* happened in the past, i.e. we can explain the event.

These informal theories are very important to us as humans, simply because we live in a world of change that is only remotely resembled in the lives of other animals. And sometimes, as models of the world, they can reach high levels of reliability, in that they have been tried and tested over countless activities and generations of time, for example navigation in a 'flat' earth; predicting planetary movements in a geocentric universe; predicting the weather from various natural phenomena. Their limitations begin to emerge only when we have to start to make decisions beyond those we have been accustomed to using the model for in the past. At such times we have to try to obtain a new and more detached view of the system that is being modelled. We have to have ways of establishing such models. And we have to have ways of establishing their veracity before we put them to common use.

Scientific theories differ from our everyday informal theories in two main ways. First, they attempt to model parts of nature beyond the here and now, or the immediately obvious. Second, they are refined, tested, and more or less agreed through the *methods* of science. Let us look at these distinctive aspects of science a little more closely.

Scientific theory

Although scientists, in their theory construction, aim to be more detached than the informal theorist this is achieved with varying degrees of success. For a start theories aren't built out of thin air. They usually originate in the informal theories that are already part of everyone's experience. These informal theories thus become incorporated into scientific theories to a greater or lesser degree. Because the former are based on subjective experience in everyday, social situations, scientific theories tend to incorporate these subjective experiences to some extent. Thus we once had scientific theories of the Earth as the centre of the universe. In a similar vein theories of intelligence are constructed which reflect the natural and 'obvious' experiences of people as they experience other people in the actual social situations in which they live: our efforts at detachment will always be dogged by such experiences.

It is important to remember this connection between the informal theories, which we all create and use in everyday life, and scientific theories which aim to be detached from them. It is the source of many confusions and controversies. Generally, of course, we aim to free our theories from such subjectivity by the use of scientific method. Let us examine how this works.

Scientific method

1 Since all science begins with a prior model, however crude, the first task is to refine this model. This means identifying the *components* of the system being

modelled; the *properties* of those components (i.e. how they behave under different conditions); and the *relations* between those properties (e.g. how changes on one component affect changes in other components).

2 None of these is likely to be immediately obvious, so special steps have to be taken to reveal them to us. As Sir Francis Bacon, the commonly acknowledged founder of the modern experimental method, put it, 'all the working of the spirits inclosed in tangible bodies lies hid and unobserved of men' (quoted in Johnston 1965: 88). This process of 'revealing' usually means taking part of the system in question and *changing* it in some way (the experimental manipulation). Components, properties and relations might then reveal themselves to us. This is the essence of the experimental method as it first arose in the sixteenth century. As Bacon further put it, 'all the truer kind of interpretation of nature is effected by instances and experiments fit and apposite' (Johnston 1965: 88) Dissection, heating, drying, applying mechanical forces, and all kinds of cunning devices are used in experiments in the natural sciences. Inducing subjects to do certain tasks, imposing certain kinds of deprivation or compensation; and getting other people to behave in certain ways towards subjects, all are ways of doing experiments in psychology. In each of these a change is being imposed on a system, so that hidden properties and relations might be revealed in a way that would not be achieved from ordinary experience or passive observation alone.

3 Having intruded on the system to get it to reveal its hidden components and properties, there are then various steps to be taken to make the business *public*. It is usually overlooked that science is a very *social* business. Yet this exposure of scientific activities to national and international comment and criticism is what most distinguishes it from the 'folklore' of informal theories. This is achieved in several ways. The procedures have to be qualified and quantified for the benefit of others, so that they may be replicated by others. In this way the procedures, instruments and measures become standardised, so that scientists anywhere in the world can check the veracity of observations and findings reported. This also implies, then, the use of universally agreed conventions about the reporting of these observations and findings.

4 As new hidden components and properties become revealed, they come to comprise a refined model or theory. This building of theories from observations is called the *inductive* aspect of science. The model should be more exact and general than its precedessor (some informal model), but the extent to which this is achieved is variable. This is a crucial matter. Theories arising from the inductive process range from the extremely fuzzy to the extremely precise. When such precision is possible the theory may be expressed as a succinct mathematical expression. The status of theories of intelligence in this regard is a matter of some controversy, with some psychologists arguing that some theories are scarcely an advance on informal theories at all, others arguing that they are extremely finely honed. Either way, having induced a new model is not the end of the matter: it has to be rigorously tested.

5 The whole point of theory construction is to improve the predictability of the system in question, as already explained. Theories are tested by testing their predictions (see Figure 1.2). First these predictions are translated in terms of noticeable or measurable changes in one (or more) components that will result from specific changes in one or more other components. This is the familiar relation between the dependent and independent variables in experiments. When this translation is complete the prediction becomes a *hypothesis*, and completes the first step in the *hypothetico-deductive* aspect of research.

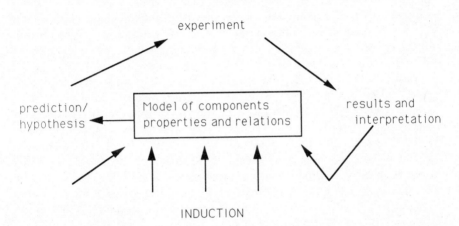

Figure 1.2 The cycle of research revolving around the construction of a theoretical model

6 A suitably formulated hypothesis is then tested by an appropriately designed experiment, which imposes the perturbation mentioned in the hypothesis while 'controlling' (holding constant) changes in other variables and measures the changes in the variables predicted. More ingenuity is usually required in experiments at this stage than in the inductive phase, simply because tighter control of properties or variables is required, and the predictions of other, rival theories have also to be ruled out. A simple correspondence between predictions and findings is in itself only weak evidence that a theory is correct, so this is a most important stipulation.

7 The findings may support the hypothesis or they may fail to support the hypothesis. In the former case the theory may be assumed to be supported. If they fail, further interpretation may suggest a fault in the experiment, and therefore a refinement to be introduced. If the theory is supported through many such experiments and replications, it may be applied to some practical problems, as mentioned previously.

This is, of course, a somewhat idealistic account of research, because what actually happens is usually more fuzzy than this. For example such a sharp distinction between inductive and hypothetico-deductive science may not be identifiable, simply because they often merge: the results of controlled experiments may themselves be inductive in so far as they lead to further theory-refinement or theory-building. And inductive investigations are always guided by prior theories, however formal or informal these may be. In practical terms the distinction really lies in the amount of control there is over clearly defined variables.

Furthermore, in areas like psychology, many additional problems present themselves. For a start, it may not even be clear what *sort* of system it is that we are trying to model or theorise. In specific areas like intelligence this creates arguments about *definition* of the system (i.e. simply describing the boundaries of the system) long before we get to the infinitely more tedious business of characterising it (i.e. describing its components, properties, etc.).

And even if we get beyond that step, it may not be possible to impose perturbations on the system in the ideal research manner, simply because of ethical considerations. In that case we simply have to gather data and induce our theories from passive observations. By the same token we may not be able to *test* theories in the strict hypothetico-deductive sense. Thus many theories in human genetics (including the genetics of intelligence) could really be settled only by human breeding experiments (Kempthorne 1978) that would be simply impossible, quite apart from grossly unethical. (Astronomy is another obvious area in which some experimental perturbations would be impractical.)

In cases like these scientists tend to rely on 'natural' experiments in which nature has, as it were, imposed the perturbation for us, and we simply monitor the consequences (e.g. children growing up in different environments, or with some specific kind of experience; in Chapter 6 we shall be discussing the study of twins as a 'natural experiment'). Or researchers can simply go on gathering as much evidence as possible inductively. If the theory is valid there will be few observations that it cannot account for, and a majority of scientists may come to be persuaded by this. Generally speaking, however, a theory can be conclusively tested only in a controlled experiment. This has produced enormous problems in the area of intelligence, as we shall see later.

What to look for in intelligence theory

We have gone into the nature of scientific theory in some depth because of what it may afford us in terms of the evaluation of theories of intelligence. A scientific theory, as opposed to an informal theory, must characterise a system in terms of its components, properties and relations. And it functions in terms of what it predicts (or, conversely, explains). The theory should ideally have been tested in experiments. And these should have been replicated several times. A good, well-tested theory will tend to attract wide agreement among scientists in the field and, *by virtue of that,* become accepted scientific knowledge. Such a theory can then safely be put into practice in the way theories are in other practical sciences such as medicine or engineering.

References

Anderson, M. (1989). New ideas in intelligence. *The Psychologist: Bulletin of the British Psychological Society,* 2: 92–4.

Craik, K. (1943). *The Nature of Explanation.* Cambridge, Cambridge University Press.

Driver, R., Guesne, E. and Tiberghien, A. (eds) (1985). *Children's Ideas in Science.* Milton Keynes, Open University Press.

Fry, P. (1984). Teachers' conceptions of students' intelligence and intelligent functioning: a cross-sectional study of elementary, secondary and tertiary level teachers. In P. Fry (ed.) *Changing Conceptions of Intelligence and Intellectual Functioning: Current Theory and Research.* Amsterdam, North-Holland.

Gentner, D. and Stevens, A.L. (eds) (1983). *Mental Models.* Hillsdale, NJ, Erlbaum.

Haldane, E.S. and Ross, G.R.T. (1931). *Descartes,* Vol. I. Cambridge, Cambridge University Press.

Hall, A.R. (1963). *From Galileo to Newton, 1630–1720.* London, Collins.

Hyman, A. and Walsh, J. (eds) (1973). *Philosophy in the Middle Ages.* Indianapolis, Hackett.

Johnson-Laird, P.N. (1983). *Mental Models.* Cambridge, Cambridge University Press.

Johnston, A. (1985). *Francis Bacon.* London, Batsford.

Kempthorne, O. (1978). Logical, epistemological and statistical aspects of nature–nurture data interpretation. *Biometrics, 34*: 1–23.

Murphy, G.L. and Medin D.L. (1985). The role of theories in conceptual coherence. *Psychologcial Review, 92*: 289–316.

Plato, *Republic,* Book III.

Richardson, K. (1988). *Understanding Psychology.* Milton Keynes, Open University Press.

Robinson, D.N. (1981). *An Intellectual History of Psychology.* New York, Macmillan.

Spencer, H. (1855). *Principles of Psychology.* London, Williams & Norgate.

Sternberg, R.J., Conway, B.E., Ketron, B.E. and Bernstein, M. (1981). People's conceptions of intelligence. *Journal of Personality and Social Psychology,* 41: 37-55.

2

Intelligence in IQ

Introduction

There are many legitimate reasons for measuring things in an area of inquiry like psychology. If, as we have just seen, science is about describing the properties and relations between components in a natural 'system', only careful measurement can reveal and summarise these with any degree of accuracy. This is part of the inductive (theory-building), hypothetico-deductive (theory-testing) process, that goes on in any science. Second, we may measure as part of the assessment of individuals in relation to particular criteria; for example the social-selection of people for particular jobs or training, or screening in medicine. Somewhat less frequently, we may want to measure as a diagnostic tool, or to provide us with some background information (i.e. a prognostic tool) in the psychological treatment of particular individuals, such as those with learning difficulties in schools. All of these uses of measurement will be mentioned in this chapter.

But the manifestation of measurement in numbers requires our careful and circumspect attention, too. Many scientists and philosophers have spoken of the power of numbers to disarm our critical faculties.

> The nature of Number . . . allows of no falsehood; for this is unrelated to them. . . . Falsehood can in no way breathe on number; for Falsehood is inimical to its nature, whereas Truth is related to and in close natural unison with . . . Number.
>
> (quoted in de Santillana 1961: 69)

So spoke the Ancient Greeks. More recently the 'power of numbers' misleadingly to justify particular social ends, especially in areas like sociology, psychology and economics, has become increasingly recognised. 'Intelligence', which can say so much about the worth or otherwise of an individual, is obviously an area where this possibility can loom large.

To say that we must know what we are measuring before we can measure is a cliché that is often neglected. Yet the difficulties of satisfying it in an area like intelligence are daunting, and often underestimated. To measure is to give us a more reliable sense of quantity than our senses alone can provide, and also a standard for comparison amongst quantities both personally and socially. This is simple enough with observable physical quantities such as length and weight: the instrument we use not only will provide reliable numbers but also parallels both the experience of our senses and the physical quantity to which it is applied.

With unobservable physical quantities we want the same parallels, but this is not so easy. Thus temperature from a thermometer gives a more reliable, or 'purified', measure than the felt 'hotness' of objects. But measure of what? Children and naive adults say it is a measure of heat, which in turn they construe as an intensive variable or entity: for example two cups of warm water added together will be construed as producing a hotter mixture of twice the temperature (Wiser 1988; Erickson and Tiberghien 1985). But this lack of differentiation between heat and temperature is wrong. As Wiser (1988: 34) notes, 'neither temperature nor felt hotness are in any ways measures of heat. Amount of heat is expressed in calories or BTUs and is measured with a calorimeter'.

What modern physicists have, of course, is a well-tested theory that relates and differentiates these 'sensed' and underlying properties: temperature (the average kinetic energy of molecules in a body) and heat (the energy exchanged by two bodies at two different temperatures). The failure to differentiate between an intensive and an interactional property leads (in children and naive adults) to many mistakes in problem-solving. According to Wiser (1988), such conceptual errors have been very common in the history of the physical sciences and have often delayed progress.

Imagine the difficulties confronting anyone who wishes to quantify and measure an attribution like intelligence. Differences in temperature at least reflect considerable agreement between people in general about what is being measured, i.e. felt 'hotness'. But this is not the case with concept of intelligence. First of all, our 'sense' of intelligence is itself an abstraction from a series or sequence of experiences; it is not directly experienced like hotness. Sensing or observing intelligence is not like observing a static or stable physical quantity, it is a cognitive impression of the dynamic process of other people's behaviour judged according to abstract and elusive criteria. Because of this, sensed intelligence is not an objective quantity in the sense that the same hotness of a body will be felt by the same humans everywhere (given a few simple conditions); what, in experience, we choose to call 'more' intelligence, and what 'less', is a social judgement that varies from people to people, employing different criteria or signals. Even experts vary considerably on such judgements and such criteria, as we shall see later.

Even if we arrive at a reliable instrument to parallel the experience of our senses, we can claim no more for it than that, without any underlying theory which relates differences in the measure to differences in some other, unobserved, phenomena responsible for those differences. Without such a theory we can never be sure that the differences in the measure that correspond with our sensed intelligence aren't due to something else, *perhaps something completely different*. The phenomenon we at first imagine may not even exist. Instead of such verification most inventors and users of measures of intelligence, as we shall see shortly, have simply constructed the source of differences in sensed intelligence as an underlying entity or force, rather in the way that children and naive adults perceive hotness as a substance, or attribute the motion of objects (as we described in Chapter 1) to a fictitious impetus. What we have in cases like temperature, of course, are collateral criteria and measures that *validate* the theory, and thus the original measures. Without these, the assumed entity remains a fiction. This proved to be the case with impetus, and with many other naive conceptions of nature, such as phlogiston (thought to account for differences in combustibility of materials) and 'bad blood' (thought to account for differences in health and disease). How much greater such fictions are likely to be with unobserved, dynamic and socially judged concepts like intelligence.

The origins of measurement

Up to the late nineteenth century there had been little attempt at measurement in intelligence, as elsewhere in psychology. But philosophers like J.S. Mill and psychologists like Bain and Spencer urged the importance of emulating the natural sciences through accurate measurements of mental life, if psychology was ever to be a true science. The first person seriously to attempt to measure intelligence was Sir Francis Galton, cousin of Charles Darwin and friend of Herbert Spencer (the latter being the first to use the term in its modern form). Like Spencer, he was not only keenly interested in the marked social grades in Britain and around the Empire, but was also convinced that these different grades were based on biologically inherited differences.

In Galton's mind, as in Spencer's, the allocation of individuals on the great social ladder, and the origins of intelligence, thus amounted to the same thing: the inevitable expression of biological 'laws'. In consequence, a person's position on the social ladder was itself a 'measure' of intelligence. Intelligence is 'natural ability', he said, and

> By natural ability, I mean those qualities of intellect and disposition, which urge and qualify a man to perform acts that lead to reputation . . . a nature which . . . will climb the path that leads to eminence, and has the strength to reach the summit.
>
> (Galton 1869: 37)

Galton's interest in measurement was not one merely of observation and theory-building, however. He already had his theory, and was keen to apply it. He protested strongly against 'pretensions of natural equality' (1869: 56), and campaigned vigorously for 'enquiry into the mental constitution of people' (quoted by Evans and Waits 1981: 41). But achieving this 'scientifically' required some systematic index or measure of natural ability.

Galton, like many before him, saw intelligence as an underlying, but pervasive, mental 'strength' or power. Because of this, he reasoned, it must also be manifested in quite simple physical or sensorimotor attributes. This would be tantamount to 'sinking a few shafts, as it were, at a few critical points'. But how were we to know that this random 'sinking of shafts' would be measuring what he claimed to be measuring? Galton's proposed strategy was to become the hallmark of the 'intelligence' test: 'In order to ascertain the best points for this purpose, the sets of measures should be compared with an independent estimate of the man's powers' (quoted by Evans and Waites 1981: 37). Thus, he asked, 'is reputation a fair test of natural ability?', and answered, 'it is the only one I can employ' (Galton 1869).

So Galton went ahead and devised tests of reaction time, discrimination in sight and hearing, judgement of length, and so on, and applied them to groups of volunteers, with the aim of obtaining a more reliable and 'pure' measure of his socially judged intelligence. But his strategy failed. There proved to be little relation between these measures and the 'independent' measure, namely people's social status.

This did not deter others from applying the same underlying rationale. An American correspondent of Galton's, J. McKeen Cattell (1890), devised an 'intelligence' test based on an even broader set of sensorimotor measures. These are indicated in the list below (cited by Miller 1962):

1 *Dynamotor pressure*   How tightly can the hand squeeze?
2 *Rate of movement*   How quickly can the hand move through a distance of 50 cms?
3 *Sensation areas*   How far apart must two points be on the skin to be recognised as two rather than one?
4 *Pressure causing pain*   How much pressure on the forehead is necessary to cause pain?
5 *Least noticeable difference in weight*   How large must the difference be between two weights before it is reliably detected?
6 *Reaction-time for sound*   How quickly can the hand be moved at the onset of an auditory signal?
7 *Time for naming colours*   How long does it take to name a strip of ten coloured papers?
8 *Bisection of a 10 cm line*   How accurately can one point to the centre of an ebony rule?
9 *Judgement of 10 sec time*   How accurately can an interval of 10 secs be judged?
10 *Number of letters remembered on once hearing*   How many letters, ordered at random, can be repeated exactly after one presentation?

Differences were found among individuals on such measures. But, again, when the measures were compared with social status it was found that there was little or no relationship. Cattell described the correlations as 'disappointingly low'.

In spite of this failure, these are, by almost universal acknowledgement, the origins of the intelligence testing movement. The most important thing to realise from this history is that it was not measurement for straightforward, objective scientific investigation. The theory was there, albeit hardly a scientific one, but one derived largely from common observation and intuition; what we described earlier as a popular or *informal* theory. And the theory had strong social implications. Measurement was devised mainly as a way of *applying* the theory in accordance with the prejudices it entailed. The 'shafts' it sunk had to agree with certain subjective *social* criteria, not scientific ones. Galton wanted the measures to underpin his eugenic breeding programme, in which, as he put it, they would serve 'for the indications of superior strains or races, and in so favouring them that their progeny shall outnumber and gradually replace that of the old one' (1883). Cattell was interested in predicting college achievement.

As such, the measures derived from this tradition, and the researchers employing them, had very little more to tell us about intelligence. They are simply numerical surrogates of something already 'known'. The scientific aim of creating or substantiating a theory with collateral measures was not the point. Given wide acceptance among psychologists of the kind of tacit theory just described, almost all of what followed in the IQ testing movement was designed to subserve social rather than scientific goals. The rest of this chapter consists of a critical look at that movement.

Binet's test

The motives behind the measurement of intelligence in the twentieth century have been predominantly social motives, not scientific ones. There were many social pressures fuelling such motives in the early years of this century. Among these was the introduction, in many countries of Europe, of systems of compulsory education. These measures brought into schools enormous numbers of children who, for whatever reasons, did not appear to be responding as hoped. There was natural concern about this. In 1904 the French Minister for Public Instruction appointed a commission to study how retarded children could best be taught. Among its recommendations was one that no child should be removed to a special school without a 'medico-pedagogical' examination to determine his or her ability to profit from teaching in an ordinary school. But how was this to be done?

A member of this commission was Alfred Binet who, with assistants Henri and Simon, had been studying child development, and ways of assessing it, for over a decade. In the light of Galton's and Cattell's failures, Binet was determined to concentrate on 'higher' mental functions. But what could these be? And how could they be measured?

Binet simply thought of all mental attributes that could possibly be quantified: memory, imagination, attention, comprehension of sentences and synonyms, aesthetic judgements, moral judgements, speed of acquiring a motor skill, and so on (see Miller 1962 for discussion). When he came to the work of the Commission, Binet already had considerable experience in devising such tests. As Miller (1962) goes on to describe the subsequent work of Binet and Simon:

> They used a large battery of mental tests, some hard, some easy. Binet collected tests from everywhere, and his own mind bubbled over with ideas for others. To discover which tests were useful, he and Simon spent endless hours in the schools with the children, watching, asking, testing, recording. Each proposed test had to be given to a large number of children. If a test did not distinguish the brighter from the duller, or the older from the younger, it was abandoned. Tests that worked were retained, even though they often failed to conform with the theoretical principles Binet and Henri had announced ten years earlier. The memory tests worked. And the tests of comprehension worked – comprehension of words, of statements, of concepts, of pictures. Binet did not retain the tests on the basis of a theory; he watched the children and let their behaviour decide which tests were good and which were irrelevant.
>
> (Miller 1962: 313)

On this basis Binet and Simon produced their first 'Metrical Scale of Intelligence' in 1905. It contained thirty items, designed for children aged 3 to 12 years, arranged in order of difficulty. They were grouped according to the proportion of a large group of children of a given age that had passed them. Here are examples of some of the items:

Imitating gestures and following simple commands
Naming objects in pictures
Repeating spoken digits
Defining common words
Drawing designs from memory
Telling how objects are alike ('similarities')
Comparing two lines of unequal length .
Putting three nouns or three verbs into a sentence
'Abstract' (comprehension) questions (e.g. 'When a person has offended you, and comes to offer his apologies, what should you do?')
Defining abstract words (by describing the difference between such words as 'boredom' and 'weariness', 'esteem' and 'friendship')
(For a fuller description of all the items see Wolf 1973: 179–83.)

The tester simply worked through the items with each child, until the latter could do no more. Performance was then compared with that expected for the age group to which the child belonged. If a child could pass half the tests expected of a 6-year-old, say, then the child was said to have a mental age of 6. Binet used the difference between the mental age and the chronological age as an index of retardation. He considered two years to be a serious deficiency (Miller 1962).

Thus was born the first modern intelligence test. Within a few years, translations were appearing in many parts of the world (for reasons mentioned above). In 1912 Stern proposed the use of the ratio of mental age to chronological age to yield the now familiar intelligence quotient or IQ:

$$IQ = \frac{\text{mental age}}{\text{chronological age}} \times 100$$

The intelligence which Binet tested

It is necesary to pause at this stage to reflect on the principles entailed in the construction of Binet's test. This is because misunderstandings about it have been the cause of so much conflict ever since, and these conflicts are, if anything, even more strong today.

Practical points

From a purely practical viewpoint, Binet's scale appeared to be a brilliant success. It was easily and quickly administered and it actually identified the children it was supposed to identify. It is doubtful whether it did this any better than, say, teachers could have done on the basis of their experience with the children (after all this was the only criterion, next to age discrimination, of acceptability of test items). But the test had an element of objectivity in that exactly the same scale was given to all children; they were therefore not being judged by any *particular* teacher, but, as it were, by teachers in general. And it afforded immediate comparability with children of the same or different ages; so that *degree* of retardation seemed to be indicated.

Theoretical points

What it was retardation *in* is quite a different point. Note that the test result provides no new *psychological* information; nothing that wasn't known about a child already. How could it? Binet largely disregarded the whole question of a model or theory about the phenomenon being assessed. Although his search for test items was systematic and painstaking, this alone does not make it scientific. As Miller (1962: 315) put it, 'he was not over-concerned with scientific purity; he had a practical problem he urgently wanted to solve, and he did whatever seemed necessary to solve it'. We have already mentioned how 'Binet did not retain the tests on the basis of a theory' and that 'they often failed to conform with the theoretical principles'.

In fact there weren't many theoretical principles available. In 1905 Binet and Simon wrote we must make known the meaning we give to this vague and very comprehensive word 'intelligence'. Almost all the phenomena that oc- cupy psychology are phenomena of intelligence. . . . There is in intel- ligence, it seems to us, a fundamental agent the lack or alteration of which has the greatest import for practical life, and that is judgement, otherwise known as good sense, practical sense, initiative, the faculty of adapting oneself. To judge well, to understand well, to reason well, these are the essential springs of intelligence.

(cited in Wolf 1973: 178)

A fundamental agent that enters into all practical life – good sense, judgement, etc: these represented no theoretical advance, since intelligence had been more or less vaguely described as such for centuries. In any case, Binet was not concerned about whether or not his test items actually matched these theoreti- cal qualities, as we have seen. His effort at measurement was not scientific research, aimed at identifying components, relations etc., as in the usual course of theory-construction and theory-testing. His purpose was entirely the practi- cal one of screening for educational retardation.

Because of the way in which items were selected for these extrinsic rather than their intrinsic (psychological) qualities, other psychologists, such as Yerkes in the USA, were quick to point out that 'Even the most enthusiastic believer in the Binet scale and methods cannot hope to maintain the thesis that at each or even at two ages precisely the same forms or aspects of human behaviour are measured' (quoted by Fancher 1985a: 122–3). Yerkes pointed out that what we really should have is a scale on which all individuals were being measured for the same thing: 'The difference', he said, was that 'between a relatively unscientific procedure and one which is striving to fulfill the essential require- ments of scientific method' (quoted by Fancher 1985a: 123).

Of course Binet *assumed* that there was a consistency in his procedures, and that what was being discriminated in children of different mental ages was the 'intelligence' he had earlier characterised more or less vaguely. And many others have made the same assumption since. But as Howe (1988a) points out, this is an error of logic. To find an IQ test a useful device, in the sense that test scores correlate with teachers' estimates, or otherwise with school perfor- mance, is one thing. Suggesting that in the Binet test performance we have identified the underlying 'cause' is quite another. Howe (1988b) likens this reasoning to declaring a factory is productive 'because it has high productivity'. But the circularity of the psychological reasoning quickly became buried be- neath the *social* reasoning that the test was subsequently used to underpin, especially in the USA.

The growth of IQ in the USA

Within a matter of years, as Miller (1962) points out, Binet's test was in use in many other parts of the world. The most rapid developments took place in the USA, where 'feeble-mindedness', especially among the new wave of immigrants, was seen to be a pressing problem from the point of view of education and national social security. Previous attempts to assess feeble-mindedness systematically had failed, as we saw earlier. All this changed when Henry H. Goddard translated Binet's test into English in 1910.

Like Galton, Goddard believed that intelligence was essentially a unitary physical or biological attribute, and that differences in it, however described, were essentially biologically inherited differences. Those who followed Goddard in the IQ testing movement have been described as staunch hereditarians who engaged in active propaganda regarding the implications of their beliefs. For instance, they advocated eugenic measures such as the sterilisation of the 'feeble-minded', a policy which was actually adopted by many states in the USA, resulting in tens of thousands of surgical operations (Pickens 1970; Karier 1972; Kamin 1974). Binet was later to protest about the Anglo-American interpretation of the test as a measure of some fixed quantity of the individual (Hunt 1961).

Their objectives, in other words, were political and social in a much more pervasive sense than Binet's. As Terman, the architect of the famous Stanford-Binet test, put it, 'If we would preserve our state for a class of people worthy to possess it, we must prevent, as far as possible, the propagation of mental degenerates' (Terman 1917). And their new tests seemed to offer the 'objective' justification of their propaganda. Chief among their targets were the new waves of immigrants pouring into the USA in the early years of the century. Eventually the IQ testers managed to ensure that every immigrant was given the IQ test as soon as they landed. The amount of 'feeble-mindedness' thus exposed soon had these psychologists pressing ardently for immigration controls, which eventually became law in 1924.

This, then, was the atmosphere in which IQ-testing grew in strength in the USA. Again, we have to stress that it was testing for *social* purposes, not scientific ones. There was no theoretical advance in this movement, no further inductive characterisation of intelligence, or hypothetico-deductive testing of theory, and little inclination to achieve any of these. But the test, with its power of number, created a mystique that won it admirers everywhere. This paradox was pointed out by Tuddenham (1962):

> Mental testing was adopted in every training school, every teacher's college in the land, and even stormed the citadels of experimental psychology on university campuses. There were few who noticed the logical flaw behind the eloquence – that the hereditary, biological intelligence that Goddard postulated and the intelligence that the tests in fact measured were *not* the same thing.
>
> (Tuddenham 1962: 45)

In the rest of this section we shall continue to look at some of the influential developments in the USA, before turning to consider what happened in Britain.

Terman's revisions of the Binet Scales

In 1916 Lewis Terman at Stanford University published the Stanford Revision of the Binet-Simon Intelligence Scale. Like the Binet test it was based on a variety of items selected according to their ability to discriminate among children in a way which agreed with a prior discrimination in terms of 'mental age', i.e. chronological age and teachers' judgements. But there were many more items (ninety in all), which therefore required more time to administer, and demanded careful instructions to test administrators. It very quickly became the 'standard' IQ test on both sides of the Atlantic. This test was revised in 1937, and again in 1960, to include a still wider variety and greater number of items. Here are examples of items which a 10-year-old would be expected to pass.

1 *Vocabulary* Correctly defining eleven words from a graded list of forty-five. The list begins with 'orange', 'envelope', 'straw', 'puddle', 'tap', and ends with 'achromatic', 'casuistry', 'homunculus', 'sudorific', and 'parterre'.
2 *Block counting* Counting the number of blocks in a three-dimensional picture in which some of the blocks are obscured (eight out of ten examples should be correct).
3 *Abstract words* Defining two of the following:

   a pity
   b curiosity
   c grief
   d surprise

4 *Finding reasons*

   a 'Give two reasons why children should not be too noisy in school.'
   b 'Give two reasons why most people would rather have a motor car than a bicycle.'

5 *Word naming* Naming as many words as possible in one minute (credit given for twenty-eight words).
6 *Repeating digits* Repeating in order at least one of the following sequences:

   a 4–7–3–8–5–9
   b 5–2–9–7–4–6
   c 7–2–8–3–9–4

For each of these, detailed scoring instructions are given, and a list of acceptable and unacceptable answers is provided. Thus, with respect to 4(a) above, acceptable answers include

Cause they'll get a lickin'. They'll have to sit in a dunce chair.

They wouldn't know what their lessons was about. Wouldn't be paying attention to teacher and wouldn't know what she was saying.

Unacceptable answers include

Because they're supposed to sit down and be still to do their studying when the teacher tells them to.

Because helps 'em out so they can study and they learn a lot when they grow up.

What makes these answers acceptable or unacceptable is that, according to the Test Manual, 'Finding reasons involves seeing the relationship between cause and effect in situations with which the child is familiar' (Terman and Merrill 1960).

The Wechsler Scales

The Wechsler Adult Intelligence Scale (WAIS) was devised in 1939 by David Wechsler and revised in 1955. He produced it in the belief that the Stanford-Binet was not very satisfactory in form or content for assessing adults. In 1949 it was augmented by the Wechsler Intelligence Scale for Children (WISC), revised in 1974, and by the Wechsler Pre-school and Primary Scale of Intelligence. For illustration, here is a brief description of the sub-scales of the WISC (used in the age range 5–15 years):

A Verbal Scale

1 *General information*   Answering questions like 'What is steam made of?' or 'What is pepper?'
2 *General comprehension*   Answering questions like 'What should you do if you see someone forget his book when he leaves his seat in a restaurant?'
3 *Arithmetic*   Solving typical school textbook problems in a given time, e.g. 'Three men divided 18 golf balls among them. How many golf balls did each man receive?'
4 *Similarities*   Describing how two things are alike, e.g. 'lion' and 'tiger', 'circle' and 'triangle'.
5 *Vocabulary*   Defining words of increasing difficulty.
6 *Digit span*   Repeating strings of numbers.

B Performance Scale

1 *Picture completion*   Identifying the missing parts in incomplete pictures.
2 *Picture arrangement*   Arranging pictures in proper order so that they tell a story.
3 *Block design*   Pictures of block structures to be reproduced by arranging coloured blocks.

4 *Object assembly*   Making a picture (e.g. a horse) out of scrambled jigsaw-like pieces.

5 *Mazes*   Tracing a way out of a maze.

The WISC and the Stanford-Binet have been far and away the most popular tests on both sides of the Atlantic, and probably are to this day. In a small survey in this country, Quicke (1982) found that these two tests were regularly used by 82 per cent and 42 per cent respectively of educational psychologists.

Theoretical evaluation

As with Binet, Terman was not concerned with the construction of a theory of intelligence that could be empirically tested, prior to application; his characterisation of intelligence was thus rough and ready. Nothing was added in theoretical terms to our understanding of intelligence. All the characteristics of the 'intelligence' revealed in the test result from assumptions built into the test itself. The first scale was assembled by selecting items, performance on which correlated with performance on the Binet Scale. The 1937 revision followed a similar routine, except this time comparing with mental ages derived from the 1916 scale.

A few further assumptions were added, however. Terman reckoned intelligence to be an all-round, 'general' power, rather like Galton had. Although a wider variety of items was used, each item was selected only if performance on it correlated to some extent with performance on the whole sample of items.

Moreover, through the process of item selection it was realised that certain differences between groups of children could be built into or built 'out of' the test. By such means, sex differences in performance in the 1916 version were later ironed out. Although a wider variety of item types was used, this was carried out on an intuitive, rather than theoretical, grounds. Although items were given a descriptive label, such as 'block counting' or 'comprehension', what these actually meant *psychologically* was another matter. As Terman himself admitted, 'Certainly, tests which bear the same label are apt to be quite different as to content and as to the kind of ability called for' (1942: 45).

It is unclear whether Wechsler added anything theoretically to our scientific understanding of intelligence. He characterised intelligence as 'the aggregate or global capacity of the individual to act purposefully, to think rationally and to deal effectively with [his or her] environment' (Wechsler 1958). But this kind of abstract generalisation – of the sort that has been around for hundreds of years –is not the same thing as the painstaking business of identifying components, properties and relations that will help reveal, and therefore validate, what we are measuring. Again Wechsler's task was to deal with a practical problem *now*, and he did so in the same pragmatic way as Binet and Terman.

This of course could be said of any scale, such as temperature or the pH scale, but it is of practical use only if we know, by virtue of an underlying theory or model (that has been adequately tested with collateral measures), what the numbers on them mean.

IQ in Britain

The Stanford-Binet test also became widely used in Britain, largely under the influence of Cyril Burt (of whom more later). Along with the WISC it came to form the standard 'tool kit' of the educational psychologist. Use of these tests has increased gradually over the years as already indicated.

The fact that by the 1960s no individual test of general intelligence had been developed in Britain had been long lamented. This situation was remedied in 1965 when a research project was set up under the auspices of the British Psychological Society to develop a test to replace the Stanford-Binet and the Wechsler scales. The stated objectives of the project were as follows:

1 the construction of a scale of general mental capacity or 'educability' adapted to British intelligence and standardised on a British population
2 the extension of the scale to a measure of special abilities.

The research team assumed intelligence to consist of an amalgam of special abilities and wanted to have this reflected in test scores. As one of the research team, Elliot (1975), explains:

> From the start, therefore, the original research team had in mind the construction of an intelligence scale which would provide a profile of special abilities rather than merely produce an overall IQ figure. The early try-out version of the scale was written with the intention of measuring a wide range of abilities, such as verbal ability, verbal fluency, numerical ability, spatial ability, inductive reasoning and memory.

And to the test-construction team, the justifications and attractions of their assumptions were simple:

> if the BIS even partially succeeds in its major aim of being a test of special abilities, it will represent a marked advance on any previously published test and hopefully will enable psychologists to define strengths and weaknesses in the abilities of a child with greater precision and with greater confidence and scientific rigour than is currently possible.
>
> (Elliot 1975: 15)

The result is claimed to be a measure of five major 'mental processes': Reasoning, Spatial Imagery, Perceptual Matching, Short-Term Memory, and Retrival and Application of Knowledge. Each of these is divided into a number of subcomponents so that in all there are 24 subscales aimed to measure 24 distinct aspects of intelligence in children between the ages of 2½–17 years. Test items include such things as (Elliot *et al.* 1978):

1 *Speed of information processing*   Each item consists of a page of a 5 × 5 block of numbers. The child has to strike out the largest number in each row. Total time is measured. Difficulty is increased from item to item by increasing the number of digits in each number, from three digits in early items to five digits in later items.

2 *Matrices*   The child has to draw in a correct solution in the blank cell as in Figure 2.1 (age range 5–17 years).

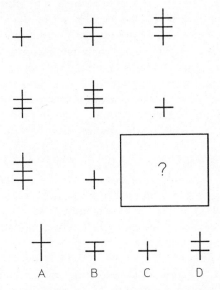

Figure 2.1   Very simple matrix item of a type found in many IQ tests.
Note: Subjects have to complete the matrix from the alternatives underneath

3 *Visualisation of cubes*   The child has to match a patterned wooden block to four drawings, only one of which accurately represents the block being held.

4 *Copying*   Copying designs and letter-like characters.

5 *Verbal-tactile matching*   Bags containing a number of objects are hung round the child's neck. There are holes in the side and the child has to find objects with stated characteristics, such as 'smooth and round'.

These are, of course, only illustrations, and their novel features should be apparent. But what are the principles on which such items are based? Again we have to examine the methods of item selection to see how these are different from traditional tests. First of all, a variety of assumptions are made about the intelligence that is now to be measured:

1 that performance on each mental or physical task is related to a specific underlying 'ability';

2 that each 'ability' varies uniformly in the population such as to form a 'latent continuum';
3 that each 'ability' is normally distributed in the population.

A further assumption is that any person's actual *performance* on a task (in this case a test item) is related solely to that person's ability and the item difficulty.

Thus test construction has depended on devising 'banks' of items of different sorts which fit this model of task performance, and which is determined by trying the items out on trial populations. (The statistical model that results from these assumptions, and which items must satisfy, is known as the Rasch model, but these technicalities need not concern us here.) The great advantage claimed for this method of item-selection is that it gives us 'direct estimates of ability', as opposed to a mere relative rank ordering of subjects. That is, 'the use of the Rasch ability scales enables us to convert a raw score into an estimate of a person's position on the latent continuum', and thus that 'Rasch ability scores have many similar characteristics to physical measurements' (Elliot *et al.* 1978: 25–6).

Unlike the Binet scales, then, the British Ability Scales are not constructed on the basis of teachers' subjective assessments; they are said to provide direct estimates of ability, as if by a dipstick or linear rule. Many have admired these innovations (e.g. Embretson 1985). But others have questioned the strong claims made of them; as Goldstein and Blinkhorn noted, 'if true, the Rasch model proposed might well be seen as the philosopher's stone of the psychometricians' (1977: 310).

There are, as yet, few grounds for knowing whether these claims are valid or not. But there are grounds for doubting whether they *can* be true. As with the Binet scales, item-selection still consists of making the test fit prior assumptions which are only crudely theorised and empirically tested. Yet all of the assumptions can be challenged.

The idea that psychologists have conveniently identified specific 'abilities' underlying performances on specific tasks is most problematic. Consider, for example, the matrix problem (Figure 2.1). These show a number of variables combining in a predictable manner, such as to allow specification of a future event (the 'missing' pattern). Yet virtually everything we do, from interpreting every sentence we hear, to crossing the road, involves just this kind of induction and deduction. We know very little about these processes (although we shall be turning to them again in Chapters 3 and 4). To give one task the label of 'ability', that we pretend is meaningful, leads us to commit the 'nominal fallacy', i.e. that naming is the same thing as characterising and explaining.

Similarly the idea that such a special ability has the underlying form of a simple physical character (like, say, height or weight), which is normally distributed in the poupulation, is problematic. A number of physical characters, in fact, are not normally distributed. Layzer (1975) instances typing speed. Micceri (1989) reports a review of over four hundred achievement and psychometric measures, the distributions of which he found to be significantly non-normal. Many other physical characters are not easily described in terms of a 'latent continuum' (for example the character of immunity to a specific disease; or the numbers of teeth, or the numbers of fingers, we have). Such assumptions may be convenient, but this doesn't make them valid.

Finally, it seems rather naive to assume that performance on a given task can be reduced to the two factors, ability and task difficulty. This may be fine for a mechanical device, such as the performance of a motor car going uphill. There has been considerable research on the effects of task performance of such human factors as anxiety, confidence, and so on (e.g. Hembree 1988). In Chapter 4 we shall also describe research implicating the crucial role of context – including the nature of the social relations in a test situation – on task performance.

In sum, although the British Ability Scales appear to use a novel approach to test *construction*, they are still, in fact, based on a number of (problematic) assumptions which the abilities of people are made to 'fit' through the processes of item selection. Construction is less blatantly pragmatic than in the Binet tests, in that measurement, superficially at least, is tailored to some underlying psychological constructs, rather than to remote criteria like 'must be easier with age', or to teachers' judgements. But there is still considerable disagreement about the existence and identity of such constructs.

Group tests

In spite of the apparent success of the Binet test the fact that is was administered by one tester to one testee at a time soon proved a major drawback. Those who would use such tests often wanted to test large numbers of people at a time, as with children in school, or recruits in the armed forces. The matter came to a head with the entry of the USA into the First World War and the persuasive-ness of Robert Yerkes over the need to test all army recruits both for mental defectiveness, and 'for the classification of men in order that they may be properly placed in the military service' (quoted by Fancher 1985a: 118). These moves resulted in two paper-and-pencil tests which could be given to people in large numbers at a time: the Army Alpha for literates, and the Army Beta for illiterates. As Fancher (1985a) notes, by early 1918 these were being admin-istered at the rate of 200,000 per month.

As with the earlier tests, construction consisted of devising batteries of items which had an intuitive correspondence with what the constructor saw as intelligence, and then selecting those which trials showed would make up a test with the required overall properties. Very soon such tests became very popular indeed. In Britain group tests were available from the early 1920s. Today many such tests are employed for personnel selection in, for instance, the Civil Service, the armed forces, and in industry. From the 1940s they were exten-sively used in educational selection. There is scarcely a person, in fact, who has not been administered such a test at one time or another.

The types of items used in group tests include the familiar range of general information, arithmetic, classification, sequences, opposites, and so on. A very common item is some type of analogy, having the general form A is to B as C is to? (select D from a range of alternatives). Matrix items are also very common in group tests. As Burt (1977) notes about such items,

> the square pattern or 'matrix' can be enlarged to include nine or even sixteen related items. . . . If lines, dots and simple geometrical figures are employed, there is hardly any limit to the material that can be systematically compiled for such purposes.
>
> (Burt 1977: 32–3)

Even the medical practitioner, interested in mental assessments, 'can get together a number of supplementary tests for himself; he will find them in many ways easier to invent, easier to apply, and often more reliable in their results than the verbal' (Burt 1977: 33). Perhaps the best known of all group tests is the Raven's Progressive Matrices, made up entirely of such items. Given the circumstances of testing, the administration of group tests is usually timed.

Criticisms of such tests echo those for individual tests, as outlined above – chiefly the intuitive rather than objective grounds for item content, and selection of items according to their surrogacy of subjective impression. How do we know differential performances on these tests, and on which individuals appear to vary, are *really* differences in intelligence? This question leads us to consider the vexed question of validity of IQ tests.

The validity of IQ tests

As defined in textbooks, the validity of a test is the extent to which it measures what it is intended to measure, but clearly there are many ways of interpreting this intention. Thus we may think a test is valid if it simply yields a measure which corresponds with a 'sensed' parameter – a thermometer in relation to sensed 'hotness', for example. On the other hand, the phenomenon to which (it is hoped) the instrument is being applied may be much more complex than this, and the major parameters not only 'hidden from view', but possibly quite different from the external impression created. It is generally agreed that validity is the most crucial quality of a psychometric test; but it has proven to be a deeply problematic issue in the IQ tradition, for the reasons just mentioned.

A measure or test is most valid when the measure in question relates to a theory which identifies the component(s) being measured in the 'system' in question, and which clearly described the causal connection between the value on a component or components and the value on that measure. Thus Newton's Laws describe a causative connection between a measure of weight and the mass of a substance being weighed. In psychometry such a connection has become known as *construct* validity. But the absence of clear theory about the intelligence we claim to be measuring has already been mentioned. So that construct validity is not one of the strengths of most IQ tests. Test designers have therefore sought other kinds of evidence about the validity of tests.

One kind of evidence evoked is the fact that IQ scores generally predict individuals' school performance fairly well. This is known as *predictive validity*. It simply reflects the purely practical quality of the tests in doing what they were originally devised to do, namely yielding a numerical correspondence with 'sensed' intelligence (without being clear about how they do it). The assumption here, of course, is that IQ tests have such predictive qualities by virtue of measuring the intelligence that it is *hoped* they measure. The question, therefore, is 'Does this make them valid as "intelligence" tests, or as tests of educational prediction?'

The validity of new tests is sometimes claimed when performances on them correlate with performances on other, previously accepted and currently used tests. This is usually called the *concurrent validity* of tests. The Stanford–Binet and the WISC are often used as the 'standards' in this respect. Whereas it may be reassuring to know that the new test appears to be measuring the same thing as an old favourite, the assumption here is that (construct) validity has already been demonstrated in the concurrent test.

Most IQ tests are unfortunately embarrassingly short on validity evidence of all kinds. For example, the Manual to the third revision of the Stanford–Binet contains but a few lines on this subject, and *no* evidence of its external validity. According to its authors, the test is valid because 'The choice of items according to mental age on the 1937 scale ensures that the new scale is measuring the same thing that was measured by the original scale' (Terman and Merrill 1960: 53). When we turn to consider the validity of the 1937 scale, however, we read:

> The item selection and procedures employed in the development of the 1937 scale also offer the chief evidence of the validity of the scale. As we have already pointed out, the preliminary selection of items was based on evidence that the items were testing the same kinds of mental functions that had proved useful in the 1916 scale.
>
> (Terman and Merrill 1961: 26)

Again no external validity is offered, nor is it in the manual to the 1916 tests, which was purely a translation of the original fifty-four Binet items, with the addition of twenty-six more devised by Terman himself. Thus the validity of the Stanford–Binet, over and above discrimination by age, lies, in the main, with the power of teachers to discriminate 'bright' and 'dull' children.

Surprisingly the term 'validity' doesn't even appear in the manual to the WISC. The validity of the British Ability Scales has been described as inadequate (e.g. Embretson 1985). Generally, wherever we look for evidence of the validity of most IQ tests, reviewers express concern about the lack of it.

In reality, the feelings of most psychologists about the validity of tests they use seems to rest on predictive correlations with school achievement and subsequent occupation level. As Jensen (1975: 346) put it, 'Intelligence tests have more than proved themselves as valid predictors of scholastic performance and occupational level'.

Correlations of IQ with school grades vary a great deal, but most fall within the range 0.4–0.6 (Block and Dworkin 1976; Brody 1985). A substantial part, at least, of such correlations is, of course, explained by the way in which items are selected precisely because performances on them correlate with performances in school, other items being rejected. 'The fact that intelligence tests correlate with academic achievement and school progress is unquestioned. From the very way in which the tests were assembled it could hardly be otherwise' (Thorndike and Hagen 1969: 325).

The predictive correlations may be self-fulfilling in another way, too. Many of the reported studies have been done on children who have already been selected and promoted in the school system on the basis of their IQ test results (Evans and Waites 1981). Or they may have been selected and promoted on the basis of superficial linguistic attributes, or social-class related aspects of knowledge, which are themselves correlated with test performances. Since school performance determines the number of years we stay at school, which in turn determines the *level* at which we enter the job market, it is, likewise, unsurprising that a correlation is found between IQ test scores and occupational level. But what about occupational *performance*? As Jensen (1970: 63) concludes, there are 'surprisingly low correlations between a wide variety of intelligence tests and actual proficiency on the job. Such correlations average about 0.20 to 0.25, and thus predict only four or five percent of the variance in work proficiency'.

Many critics have thus doubted the value of such 'achievement' correlations as evidence of the validity of IQ tests. McClelland (1973: 2), after a review of such data, concluded that 'the testing movement is in grave danger of perpetuating a mythological meritocracy in which none of the measures of merit bears significant demonstrable validity with respect to any measure outside of the charmed circle'. And Goodnow (1986) has called for a closer examination of assumptions involved in interpreting such predictions:

> If we are to test for something, we should clearly have a clearer sense of what that something is. . . . Why not a moratorium until we know more clearly what we are trying to predict, and what the costs and benefits are of various ways of proceeding?
>
> (Goodnow 1986: 88)

Finally, we have to remember that a correlation is not direct evidence of a cause. The correlation between IQ and school performance may be a *necessary* aspect of the validity of the tests, but it is not a *sufficient* one. Such evidence, as already mentioned, requires a clear connection between a theory (a model of intelligence), and the values on the measure. Without such a connection, correlations may be explained in a variety of alternative ways (see Howe 1988a; 1988b).

Testers and test-constructors respond to these problems in various ways. One response is to warn that test scores should not be interpreted beyond the very narrow practical purpose for which they were invented (e.g. prediction of school performance). Acknowledging this warning really means viewing an 'intelligence' test strictly as a 'scholastic prediction' test, and nothing more. Another response has been to attempt to relax some of the traditional demands about test validity. There is considerable debate about these matters at the present time; we could not hope to resolve them here.

Theorising intelligence on the basis of test scores

Intelligence testing grew as a technology rather than a science. Behind it, of course, were certain ideas that found expression in grandiloquent statements. But when we refer to Binet's theory or Terman's theory or Wechsler's theory, we are talking only of *informal* theory, in the sense referred to in the previous chapter, and not to systematically constructed, well-tested scientific theory. In fact, the general effect of test scores upon the reasoning of psychologists has been one of intense puzzlement about what they actually mean.

The question 'What *is* intelligence?' is one which has plagued the psychometric approach. As pointed out several times above, IQ testing arose without anyone having a clear answer to this question. There is an obvious contradiction in claiming to measure something when we aren't very clear about what it is. Throughout the twentieth century efforts have been made to rationalise this problem through *post hoc* characterisations. Most efforts have been devoted to the question of *defining* intelligence. Definition, of course, is not the same as theoretical characterisation of a phenomenon; rather it is a way of saying, 'Let's first get a rough idea of what it is we are talking about, so that we know what questions to start asking about it'.

This problem first came to light in a symposium in 1921 in which the editors of the *Journal of Educational Psychology* asked those prominent in the area of intelligence at that time to state what they considered 'intelligence' to be, and by what means it could be best measured by group tests. The diversity of answers received, and the absence of agreement among them, have been famous ever since. They led to the half-joking, half-exasperated claim that 'intelligence is what intelligence tests test' (Boring 1923).

This exercise has recently been repeated by Detterman and Sternberg (1986). They wrote to a couple of dozen theorists, asking them the same questions that were put to the experts in 1921. Sternberg and Berg (1986) analysed the results for frequencies of mentioned attributes. Of the twenty-five attributes mentioned in 1986, only three were mentioned by 25 per cent or more of respondents (half of the respondents mentioned 'higher level components'; 25 per cent mentioned 'executive processes'; and 29 per cent mentioned 'that which is valued by culture'). Over a third of the attributes were mentioned by fewer than 10 per cent of respondents in each case. The responses are in some ways similar to those given in the 1921 survey; for example 21 per cent of respondents mentioned 'elementary processes (perception, sensation, attention)' as part of the definition of intelligence in both surveys. But there are some striking differences; for example only 8 per cent of the 1986 respondents mentioned 'ability to learn', compared with 29 per cent in 1921.

These responses generally reveal a motley collection of ideas in both periods. The problem of agreement about where the boundaries of intelligence lie is obviously still with us.

Charles Spearman and the arguments about '*g*'

Galton had viewed intelligence as an all-pervasive 'natural ability'. Binet had viewed it as a kind of amalgam — some were to say a 'hotchpotch' — of some vague abilities such as judgement, reasoning, good sense, and so on. Charles Spearman (see Spearman 1904) shared Galton's hunch, and attempted to turn it into a respectable scientific theory by examining the statistical interrelations of intellectual performances of various kinds. Since much of what follows — and indeed much else about theory in intelligence — is based on the ubiquitous correlation coefficient, it is probably worth spending a little more time on this statistic first.

A correlation is the tendency for one measure to covary with another: for instance, height and weight tend to covary in that individuals who tend to vary to a certain degree from the average on height also tend to vary from the average to a similar degree in weight. This is called a positive correlation, because the covariation is in the same direction. A negative correlation can arise when the covariation is in the opposite direction: for example, between sunshine and rainfall across counties of England.

Karl Pearson, an associate of Galton's, building on some of Galton's earlier work, developed a measure of correlation based on the degree of covariation between measures. This was expressed as a proportion from 0 to 1 for a positive correlation, or 0 to −1 for a negative correlation. This is the statistic with which Spearman worked (and also modified and adapted in some ways). Before going on to consider this work note two crucial points. First the correlation is a measure of the degree to which two measures *vary together* from the average: it is not a measure of similarity, let alone of identity, in what is being measured. Thus pairs of test scores, say, may be highly correlated without them necessarily being very similar. Second, a correlation does not in itself imply some necessary path of causation between the measures. Commentators are frequently pointing out to students that measures may covary almost perfectly (e.g. the population of the Earth and the price of coffee over the last few years) without any causal connection between them. Unfortunately this oft-repeated missive frequently becomes forgotten.

So far we have been talking about correlation between two measures. It is also possible to measure the correlation between three or more measures. This brings us to Spearman's studies. Spearman's first (1904) investigation was conducted on twenty-four children in a village school. He obtained three different indices of performance:

1 Teacher's ranking of the group for their 'cleverness in school':
2 The two oldest children's ranking of the group for 'sharpness and common sense out of school';
3 Spearman's ranking of the children on pitch-, light- and weight-discrimination.

He reported that the three indices of performance correlated with each other to the value of 0.55 (i.e. a moderate degree of covariation across the group). The correlation between the 'intellectual' and sensory measures was 0.38. After applying a correction he had devised for 'attenuation' (or depression of correlations resulting from the unreliability of the indices as measures) Spearman reached the remarkable conclusion that the 'true' correlation between 'intellectual' and sensory measures was in the region of 1.0, which is the value expected of an all-pervasive mental factor.

Much encouraged by this confirmation of Galton's ideas, he conducted a second study on twenty-two boys from a preparatory school. This time he took examination grades in Classics, French, English and Maths, corrected for age, and correlated them with a pitch-discrimination task and a teacher's rankings of the boys on musical proficiency (see Fancher 1985a and 1985b for description and discussion). Again he found the corrected or true correlation between 'intellectual' and sensory measures to be around the value of 1.0 expected of a general factor. Thus he reached the conclusion 'That *there really exists a something that we may provisionally term . . . "General Intelligence"* ' quoted by Fancher 1985b: 342, Spearman's emphasis).

Thus Spearman envisaged a unitary, general factor (which he called *g*) in intelligence, which is expressed in different activities to different degrees, the particular activities being also determined by specific (or *s*) factors. This is known to this day as the famous 'two-factor' theory. Spearman himself was cock-a-hoop with the idea. Declaring that it signalled a 'Copernican revolution' in psychology, he went on to argue, 'In these principles we must venture to hope that the long missing genuinely scientific foundation for psychology has at last been supplied' (1923: 355, c.f. Gould 1981). Psychologists from Burt (1909) to Jensen (1969) have hailed it as perhaps the most important discovery in the whole field of intelligence testing.

Spearman went on to develop the notion in his later works (Spearman 1923; 1927). Irvine (1987) notes Spearman's anxiety about transforming the entire field into an exact science like physics, and thereby saw, in his scores and assessments, different manifestations of one and the same thing, a quasi-mechanical mental force. As Spearman himself explained,

The (*g*) factor was taken, pending further information, to consist in something of the nature of an 'energy' or 'power' which serves in common the whole cortex (or possibly, even, the whole nervous system). But if, thus, the totality of cognitive operations is served by some general factor in common, then each different operation must necessarily be further served by some *specific* factor peculiar to it. For this factor also, a physiological substrate has been suggested, namely, the particular group of neurons specially serving the particular kind of operation. These neural groups would thus function as alternative 'engines' into which the common supply of 'energy' could be alternatively distributed.

> (quoted in Fancher 1985a; 95)

The two-factor theory of intelligence (which, as Butcher 1968 notes, could more accurately have been called a 'one-factor' theory), involving a general factor and special factors, each of which is more or less 'saturated' with *g*, is still strongly favoured to this day. It has survived, though, in the face of many criticisms. Among these are the empirical criticisms. Thus replications of Spearman's studies have usually shown low correlations between 'intellectual' and sensory measures, and lower intercorrelations among different intellectual performances (see Fancher 1985a and 1986b for details).

Much stronger, however, is the logical criticism – that the mere demonstration of substantial correlation among performances may be a *necessary* requirement of a general factor, but it is not a *sufficient* one. A variety of non-intellectual (e.g. attentional or motivational) factors could also produce such correlations. Moreover, it is possible for quite independent factors to produce a hierarchy of correlations without the existence of any underlying 'general' factor (Fancher 1985a; Richardson and Bynner 1984).

This whole tendency to imagine underlying causes or unseen agents in patterns of correlations, where in fact there may well be none, is known as reification. As Gould (1981) explains, Spearman's inference that there really is a 'something' was a cardinal error:

> He reified it as an 'entity' and tried to give it an unambiguous causal interpretation. He called it *g*, or general intelligence, and imagined that he had identified a unitary quality underlying all cognitive mental activity – a quality that could be expressed as a single number and used to rank people on a unilinear scale of intellectual worth.
>
> (Gould 1981: 251)

From this reification Spearman went on to assert the essential hereditary nature of *g*, and this unitary concept as the only theoretically justifiable basis of the measurement of intelligence. He consequently ridiculed IQ testing of the kind reviewed in the previous section as utterly without the scientific foundation that only his own theory could furnish (see Gould 1981). But Spearman's reification was not the end of the story. He went on to do further analyses of correlations of a sort which became known as 'factor-analysis'. This became the beginning of a much bigger story.

Factor analysis and the structure of intelligence

The most influential psychologist in the making of this story was Cyril Burt. As an admirer of Spearman and Galton, he too held a prior belief in the unitary, and hereditary, nature of intelligence. He carried out studies similar to those of Spearman (though on even smaller numbers of subjects) and arrived at similar results and conclusions, namely that intelligence is a unitary 'force', as Galton had decreed, and that it occurs in individuals to a degree that is determined by heredity: thus 'innate, general, cognitive ability' (Burt 1955).

Burt went on to devise means of conducting further analyses on sets of scores obtained from diverse tests in the manner of Spearman. This is what became known as the method of factor anlaysis. It has been both productive and controversial. This is not the place for a full technical account of the method of factor analysis (students are referred to the excellent account given by Gould 1981). Rather a glimpse of its essentials and of the kinds of interpretations it leads to are all that can be aimed for. First, we shall attempt to give a sketch of the procedure, and then consider some criticisms.

Spearman's reasoning was that performances which correlate significantly are probably only attenuated expressions of a single 'underlying' variable or 'factor'. Factor analysis extends this kind of interpretation. Thus a substantial correlation between two measures can be reduced to a single 'factor' with little loss of information. If this applies to two measures then it can be applied to several, though greater amounts of information can now be lost. Factor analysis is about finding compromises between the identification of common underlying 'factors' and the minimisation of the loss of information in the separate measures.

The technique is performed on tables of correlations such as that produced by Spearman (Table 2.1). The first, or general, factor might account for most of the information in the set of intercorrelations, as Spearman thought – or it might not. Once this information has been accounted for, other residual

Table 2.1 Spearman's reported correlations among scholastic and sensory measures

	1	2	3	4	5	6
1 Classics						
2 French	0.83					
3 English	0.78	0.67				
4 Maths	0.70	0.67	0.64			
5 Pitch	0.66	0.65	0.54	0.45		
6 Music	0.63	0.57	0.51	0.51	0.40	

correlations may remain, suggesting other, perhaps subsidiary, factors. These in turn may then be 'removed' to see if other factors are evident, and so on until the residual correlations are statistically non-significant.

This sounds like an extremely powerful technique, but there is a snag. This is that there may be a large number of ways of solving any given pattern of correlations: a great deal of subjective judgement, many assumptions, and, of course, presuppositions about the nature of intelligence are required in deciding what is and is not a 'factor'. In consequence, a variety of 'structures of intelligence' have been proposed. Burt himself eventually came to identify a more hierarchical structure than Spearman's, with additional levels of group factors of increasing specificity. This view was famously expressed in a diagram by Vernon (1950 – see Figure 2.2). After the *g* or general factor is removed, two broad group factors appear, which have been described, from inspection of the items producing them, as verbal-educational (v-ed) and spatial-mechanical (k-m) factors. After the effects of these factors have been removed other, more specific, factors appear, which have been more or less vaguely identified, so that the resulting diagram is intended as a rough guide rather than a precise depiction of reality.

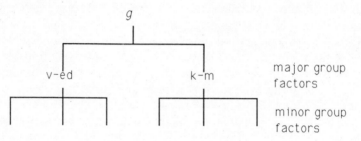

Figure 2.2   Hierarchical factor structure of IQ test scores according to one form of analysis
Source: Modified from Vernon 1950

The hierarchical view developed in Britain became known as the 'London line'. Remember how it stemmed from the beliefs of Spearman and Galton of intelligence as a unitary 'force'. Some American psychologists, however, tended to favour the Binet view of intelligence as a constellation of several different abilities. Using somewhat different assumptions, and thus different computations, from those in the London line, Thurstone (1938) arrived at results indicating seven separate factors in test scores, rather than a general factor and sub-factors. These were described as:

S – spatial ability
P – perceptual ability
N – numerical ability
V – verbal ability

M – memory
W – verbal fluency
I   – inductive reasoning

On the basis of these analyses Thurstone devised a new test known as the Primary Mental Ability Test, which emphasised this different structure of intelligence. This was reckoned to provide a profile of the separate mental strengths of individual children, without the need to admit a 'general intelligence'. (Even though, as Thurstone was later to admit, the fact that scores on these factors tended to intercorrelate *implied* a more general factor, and the published tests subsequently provided instructions for estimating a general intelligence score!)

A number of other psychologists at this time were looking afresh at the 'structure of intelligence' and seeing different things. One of these is R.B. Cattell, who declared that 'in the mid-thirties some half dozen different lines of evidence converged in the present writer's thinking to suggest the disturbing idea that *g* might be two general factors instead of one!' (1971: 74).

Again using elaborate forms of factor analysis, Cattell arrived at a distinction between a 'fluid' intelligence and a 'crystallised' intelligence.

> One of these powers – that unconnected with cultural skills, which rises at its own rate and falls despite cultural stimulus and which is affected in no specific behavioural area by brain injury – has the 'fluid' quality of being directable to almost any problem. By contrast, the other is invested in particular areas of crystallised skills which can be upset individually without affecting the others.
>
> (Cattell 1971: 80)

Thus Cattell claimed that 'fluid' intelligence was not related to content of task and devised tests (involving items like series completion, analogies and classification, which we encountered earlier) which he said were 'culture-free'. This claim, in itself, is one which has generated a great deal of controversy, and we shall return to it in Chapter 4.

The burgeoning of separate factors reached a climax in Guilford's (1959) 'Structure of Intellect Model'. Guilford factor-analysed test data from large samples of individuals and Thurstone's eight factors were increased to about forty. 'By that time', as Guilford (1985) put it, 'certain similarities and differences among the abilities were standing out, as were some parallels; thus an attempt was made to organise them' (1985: 229). And so it has gone on.

These famous examples illustrate the results of factor analysis of test scores. Even in their mutual contradictions they have been extremely influential about the structure of intelligence. As Butcher (1968: 43) put it, 'the views at the present time about this structure have been more strongly influenced by the results of factor analysis than by any other approach'. The pitfalls need to be mentioned again and again, however, because they are very easily forgotten.

Thus in one acount Burt (1977) gives the following warning about equating 'factors' with the 'faculties' of mind that were commonly identified in the nineteenth century:

> The old-fashioned faculties were pictured as completely independent entities, lodged in separate organs or areas of the brain; the specific factors of the modern psychologist are simply abstract constituents deduced by statistical analysis: it is conceivable that they have no more concrete existence than the north and south poles . . . the so-called specific factor is no more than a convenient name for a relatively general tendency.
>
> (Burt 1977: 40)

Yet only a few pages earlier, Burt had waxed enthusiastically:

> The method of correlation has been applied to almost every mental quality that can be measured, tested or assessed. The results are of immediate practical significance. It appears, for example, that many characteristics go together in groups . . . 'key factors' governing the detailed make-up of each individual mind.
>
> (Burt 1977: 21)

The influence of factor analysis on people's views of intelligence is probably just as strong today. But the arguments continue about the arbitrariness of the approach; about the fact that you can get as many different structures out as assumptions you are prepared to put in; that none is demonstrably more valid than the other (see Bynner and Romney 1986; Richardson and Bynner 1988); and of the dangers of reification. The beliefs of psychologists in this area, however, die hard as the following claims, taken from the same volume, illustrate:

> Psychometric studies have now pretty well resolved this dispute: there clearly is need for a general factor to account for the 'positive manifold' usually produced when IQ scores are intercorrelated.
>
> (Eysenck 1986: 3)

> There are good reasons for discounting the idea that there is a single, unitary capacity of general intelligence. Most of the evidence before us suggests that humans have several different intellectual capacities for which there is no functionary unity – or if there is, it has yet to be defined.
>
> (Horn 1986: 35)

Even these general cautions, however, have to be reinforced by other peculiarities of the measure itself. Remember, for example, that IQ test scores are not ordinary (random) multivariate data, but arise from batteries of items that, themselves, have been subjected to considerable pre-selection (using criteria and procedures that we have already described). Are investigators involved in such analyses, therefore, studying the 'structure' of intelligence or the structure of intelligence test scores? These may be two quite different things. Although diagrams like those presented above frequently appear in student textbooks, the 'structures' they represent have no more tangible status than the factors themselves. The very diversity of depiction should be sufficient to warn of their conjectural nature, although they are often treated in the literature on intelligence as 'hard' knowledge.

Further theoretical efforts

Theorists within the IQ tradition generally agree that they are measuring some underlying pervasive strength or mental force. But definition has proved elusive and the strategy of *post hoc* factorising of test scores has proved uncertain. Here we consider a few other attempts to characterise intelligence in theoretical terms, again to provide illustrations of the diversity of formulation, rather than an exhaustive account.

As we have seen, Spearman was among the first this century to conjecture intelligence as 'something in the nature of an "energy" or "power" which serves the whole cortex' (quoted by Fancher 1985a: 95). But probably more than any other psychologist in the IQ tradition, Spearman was interested in constructing an experimentally based *theory* of intelligence. So he continued his efforts to characterise this force, albeit largely by intellectual rather than empirical means. His beliefs were set down in his 1923 book, *The Nature of 'Intelligence' and the Principles of Cognition*. The following quotations reflect his amplifications of g at that time:

> Everything intellectual can be reduced to some special case . . . of educing either relations or correlates.

> The eduction of relations . . . when a person has in mind any two or more ideas . . . he has more or less power to bring to mind any relations that exist between them.

> The eduction of correlates . . . when a person has in mind any ideas together with a relation, he has more or less power to bring up into mind the correlative idea. For example, let anyone hear a musical note and try to imagine the note a fifth higher.

These were not, even then, new ideas. They reiterate formulations expressed centuries ago, as we saw in Chapter 1. But the real difficulty lies in building a respectable cognitive model of these procedures, such that this 'power to bring up into mind' can be expressed in hypothetico-deductive terms that can, in turn, be rigorously tested. Only in such ways can the unobserved 'system' be clarified; and only in such ways can we know that differences in the measure we call IQ really correspond with quantitative differences in that system and in nothing else. As mentioned in Chapter 1, such theory-elaboration and hypothesis-generation is a formidably difficult task in a complex, uncharted area like cognitive functions; but it is one we all have to confront sooner or later. Certainly Spearman and his colleagues in the 1920s spent a great deal of time devising test items such as analogies and matrices that might measure the power they had proposed. But no greater theoretical elaboration emerged.

Similar problems are found in other generalised statements about the 'nature' of intelligence. For example, Burt (1949) described a hierarchical structure of intelligence consisting of group factors (including sensory, perceptual, associative and relational factors) on several levels. Vernon (1979) following Hebb (1949) made a distinction between Intelligence A, Intelligence B and Intelligence C – 'A' being the biological substratum of Intelligence, 'B' being that which is manifested in our actual behaviour, and 'C' being that which is measured in an IQ score. Although some people have found these distinctions useful, again they are not expressed in the form of detailed theory.

Is there intelligence in IQ?

The measurement of intelligence in the twentieth century arose partly out of attempts to 'prove' or justify a particular world view, and partly for purposes of screening and social selection. It is hardly surprising that its subsequent fate has been one of uncertainty and controversy, nor that it has raised so many social and political issues (see, for example, Joynson 1989 for discussion of such issues). The method of devising a 'measure' – that of inventing and selecting tasks, performance on which agreed with other 'signs' of intelligence – 'worked' in its manifestation in the Binet test. But this has incurred costs of another kind. The major cost of this success is that no one has been at all sure about what is being measured. In consequence the technical validity of IQ tests is piecemeal, to say the least; and their predictive quality in educational achievement merely a reflection of the way the original tests were created on the basis of teachers' judgements of children's 'intelligence'. IQ has little if any predictive strength in relation to subsequent *occupational* performance.

Attempts to theorise intelligence on the basis of test scores have been based on *post hoc* correlational and factor analytical methods. The fallacies of reification, as well as the subjective elements in such methods, have frequently been pointed out, and in fact are starkly displayed in the diverse 'structures' that have been proposed for intelligence. Attempts to characterise intelligence, in fact, seem to have added little to speculations stretching back centuries.

The illustrations given above will, perhaps, have indicated the difficulties of theorising in this manner. The failure to do so with any clarity or consensus, in fact, has led to increasing disappointment with the whole approach, in recent years. As Eysenck (1986: 4) explains, the emphasis on Binet-type scores led 'to a neglect of theoretical and experimental investigations of intelligence and hence to the (largely justified) accusation that intelligence testing is a technology not based on proper scientific foundations'.

As a result there has been a shift in research away from test-focused to 'process-focused' theories (Horn 1986). These are what we take up in the next chapter.

References

Binet, A. and Simon, T. (1905). Méthodes nouvelles pour le diagnostic du niveau intellectuel des anormaux. *L'Année Psychologique*, 11: 191–244.

Block, N. and Dworkin, G. (eds) (1976). *The IQ Controversy*. New York, Pantheon.

Boring, E.G. (1923). Intelligence as the tests test it. *New Republic*, June, 35–7.

Brody, N. (1985). The validity of tests of intelligence. In B.B. Wolman (ed.) *Handbook of Intelligence*. New York, Wiley.

Burt, C. (1949). The structure of the mind: a review of the results of factor analysis. *British Journal of Educational Psychology*, 19: 176–99.

—— (1955). The evidence for the concept of intelligence. *British Journal of Educational Psychology*, 25: 158–77.

—— (1977). *The Subnormal Mind*. Oxford, Oxford Univesity Press.

Burt, C.L. (1909). Experimental tests of general intelligence. *British Journal of Psychology*, 3: 94–17.

Butcher, H.J. (1968). *Human Intelligence: Its Nature and Assessment*. London, Methuen.

Bynner, J.M. (1988). *Validity Coefficients*. Occasional Papers, 88/4, Centre for Human Development and Learning. The Open University.

Bynner, J.M. and Romney, D. (1986). Intelligence, fact or artefact: alternative structures for cognitive abilities. *British Journal of Educational Psychology*, 56: 13–23.

Cattell, J. McK. (1890). Mental tests and measurement. *Mind*, 15: 373–80.

Cattell, R.B. (1971). *Abilities: Their Structure, Growth and Action*. Boston, Mass., Houghton Mifflin.

de Santillana, G. (1961). *The Origins of Scientific Thought*. New York, Mentor Books.

Detterman, D.K. and Sternberg, R.J. (eds) (1986). *What is Intelligence? Contemporary Viewpoints on its Nature and Definition*. Norwood, NJ, Ablex.

Driver, R., Guesne, E. and Tiberghien, A. (1985). Children's ideas and the learning of science. In R. Driver, E. Guesne and A. Tiberghien (eds) *Children's Ideas in Science*. Milton Keynes, Open University Press.

Elliot, C.D. (1975). The British Intelligence Scale takes shape. *Education*, 25: 460–5.

Elliot, C.D., Murray, D. and Pearson, L.S. (1978). *The British Ability Scales*. Windsor: NFER.

Embretson (Whitely), S. (1985). Review of the British Ability Scales. In J.V. Mitchell jr. (ed.) *The Ninth Mental Measurements Yearbook*, vol. 1. Lincoln, Nebr., University of Nebraska Press.

Erickson, G. and Tiberghien, A. (1985). Heat and temperature. In R. Driver, E. Guesne and A. Tiberghein (eds) *Children's Ideas in Science*. Milton Keynes, Open University Press.

Evans, B. and Waites, B. (1981). *IQ and Mental Testing: An Unnatural Science and its Social History*. London, Macmillan.

Everitt, B.S. and Dunn, G. (1983). *Advanced Methods of Data Exploration and Modelling*. London, Heinemann.

Eysenck, H.G. (1986). The theory of intelligence and the psychophysiology of cognition. In R.J. Sternberg (ed.) *Advances in the Psychology of Human Intelligence*, vol. 3. Hillsdale, NJ, Erlbaum.

Fancher, R.E. (1985a). *The Intelligence Men: Makers of the IQ Controversy*. New York, Norton.

—— (1985b). Spearman's original computation of *g*: a model for Burt? *British Journal of Psychology*, 76: 341–352.

Galton, F. (1869). *Heredity Genius: An Inquiry into its Laws and Consequences*. London, Macmillan.

—— (1883). *Inquiry into Human Faculty and its Development*. London, Macmillan.

Goldstein, H. and Blinkhorn, S. (1977). *Monitoring Educational Standards – an inappropriate model*. Bulletin of the British Psychological Society, 30: 309–11.

Goodnow, J.J. (1986). A social view of intelligence. In D.K. Detterman and R.J. Sternberg (eds) *What is Intelligence? Contemporary Viewpoints on its Nature and Definition*. Norwood, NJ, Ablex.

Gould, S.J. (1981). *The Mismeasure of Man*. New York, Norton.

Guilford, J.P. (1959). Three faces of intellect. *American Psychologist*, 1,114: 459–79.

—— (1985). The structure of intellect model. In B.B. Wolman (ed.) *Handbook of Intelligence*. New York, Wiley.

Hebb, D.O. (1949). *The Organisation of Behaviour*. New York, Wiley.

Hembree, R. (1988). Correlates, causes, effects, and treatment of test anxiety. *Review of Educational Research*, 58: 47–77.

Horn, J. (1986). Intellectual ability concepts. In R.J. Sternberg (ed.) *Advances in the Psychology of Human Intelligence*, vol. 3. Hillsdale, NJ, Erlbaum.

Howe, M. (1988a). Intelligence as explanation. *British Journal of Psychology*, 79: 349–60.

—— (1988b). Explaining away intelligence. *British Journal of Psychology*, 80: 539–45.

Hunt, J, McV. (1961). *Intelligence and Experience*. New York, Ronald Press.

Irvine, S.H. (1987). Functions and constants in mental measurement: a taxonomic approach. In S.H. Irvine and S.E. Newstead (eds) *Intelligence and Cognition: Contemporary Frames of Reference*. Dordrecht, Martinus Nijhoff (in co-operation with NATO Scientific Affairs Divison).

Jensen, A.R. (1969). How much can we boost IQ and scholastic achievement? *Harvard Educational Review*, 39: 1–123.

—— (1970). Another look at culture-fair testing. In J. Hellmuth (ed.) *The Disadvantaged Child*. New York, Brunner-Mazel.

—— (1975). Race, intelligence and genetics: the differences are real. In J.M. Whitehead (ed.) *Personality and Learning*. London and Milton Keynes, Hodder and Stoughton in association with Open University Press.

Joynson, R.B. (1989). *The Burt Affair*. London, Routledge.

Kamin, L. (1974). *The Science and Politics of IQ*. New York, John Wiley.

Karier, C.J. (1972). Testing for order and control in the corporate liberal state. *Educational Theory*, 22: 154–80.

Layzer, D. (1973). Science or superstition? A physical scientist looks at the IQ controversy. *Cognition*, 1: 2,265–300.

McClelland, D.C. (1973). Testing for competence rather than for 'intelligence'. *American Psychologist*, 28: 1–14.

Micceri, T. (1989). The unicorn, the normal curve, and other improbable creatures. *Psychological Bulletin*, 25: 156–66.

Miller, G.A. (1962). *Psychology: The Science of Mental Life*. Harmondsworth, Penguin.

Pickens, E. (1970). *Eugenics and the Progressives*. New York, Vanderbilt University Press.

Quicke, J.C. (1982). *The Cautious Expert*, Milton Keynes, Open University Press.

Richardson, K. and Bynner, J.M. (1984). Intelligence: past and future. In P.S. Fry (ed.) *Changing Conceptions of Intelligence and Intellectual Functioning*. Amsterdam, North-Holland.

Spearman, C. (1904). 'General Intelligence', objectively determined and measured. *American Journal of Psychology*, 15: 201–99.

—— (1923). *The Nature of 'Intelligence' and the Principles of Cognition*. London, Macmillan.

—— (1927). *The Abilities of Man: Their Nature and Measurement*. New York, Macmillan.

Sternberg, R.J. and Berg, C.A. (1986). Quantitative integration: definitions of intelligence: a comparison of the 1921 and 1986 symposia. In D.K. Detterman and R.J. Sternberg (eds) *What is Intelligence? Contemporary Viewpoints on its Nature and Definition*. Norwood, NJ. Ablex.

Terman, L.M. (1916). *The Measurement of Intelligence*. Boston, Mass., Houghton Mifflin.

—— (1917). Feeble minded children in the public schools of California. *School and Society*, 5: 161–5.

—— (1942). The revision procedures. In Q. McNemar (ed.) *The Revision of the Stanford-Binet Scale*. Boston, Mass., Houghton Mifflin.

Terman, L.M. and Merrill, M.A. (1969). *Stanford Binet Intelligence Scale. Manual for the Third Revision, Form L-M*. Boston, Mass., Houghton Mifflin.

Thorndike, R.L. and Hagen, E.P. (1969). *Measurement and Evaluation in Psychology and Education*. New York, Wiley.

Thurstone, L.L. (1938). *Primary Mental Abilities*, Psychometric Monographs No. 1.

Tuddenham, R.D. (1962). The nature and measurement of intelligence. In L. Postman (ed.) *Psychology in the Making*. New York, Knopf.

Vernon, P.E. (1950). *The Structure of Human Abilities*. London, Methuen.

—— (1979). *Intelligence, Heredity and Environment*. San Francisco, Freeman.

Wechsler, D. (1958). *The Measurement and Appraisal of Adult Intelligence*. Baltimore, NJ, Williams & Wilkins.

Wiser, M. (1988). The differentiation of heat and temperature: history of science and novice–expert shift. In S. Strauss (ed.) *Ontogeny, Phylogeny and Historical Development*. Norwood, NJ, Ablex.

Wolf, T.H. (1973). *Alfred Binet*. Chicago, Ill., University of Chicago Press.

3

Intelligence in cognition

Introduction

We saw at the end of the previous chapter how and why there have been so many disappointments with the psychometric (IQ) approach. As Keating and MacLean (1987) note, 'Understanding how inter- and intra-individual differences in performance come to exist thus lies beyond psychometric theory, and requires a different approach' (1987: 247). This has led to demands for a return to a more 'theoretical and experimental' approach, and for more 'process-focused' theories; in other words for 'reductionist attempts to define the abilities of intelligence in terms of basic, essential capacities, rather in the way a physical scientist describes matter in terms of atoms' (Horn 1986: 43).

This implies a move to a more conventional logic of theory induction and hypothetico-deductive experimental testing, as outlined in Chapter 1. In this chapter we shall review the results of this move, and evaluate the extent to which it has obtained its scientific goals.

Intelligence as information processing

The search for basic processes as the constituents of intelligence has inevitably turned investigators' attention to the observations and theories of cognitive psychology. 'During the past decade or so, investigators of intelligence have tended to emphasise understanding of the cognitive basis of intellectual functioning' (Sternberg 1986: xiii). This has meant, by and large, attempting to construct theoretical descriptions of intelligence in terms of 'information processing'.

The roots of this approach, in cognitive psychology generally, lie in the advent of the computer, the storage and manipulation of data in which seem rather like human cognition. 'Cognitive psychology and cognitive science . . . have taken the computational metaphor to heart. The metaphor may be expressed thus: The mind is governed by programs or sets of rules analogous to those which govern computers' (Casey and Moran 1989: 148). Thus there has been a tendency to think of human intelligence as it is in an 'intellectual' computer. As Kail and Pellegrino (1985) explain:

In effect the information processing perspective leads one to ask questions about human problem solvers that are analogous to those we would ask about the computer. We would attempt to discover the processes (routines) that are required to solve the problem and to identify the strategy or plan (executive routine) that integrates specific processes into a functional package that produces the desired results.

(Kail and Pellegrino 1985: 53–4)

Cognitive theorists have tended to identify, within the cognitive system, two major aspects of information processing: the knowledge base; and the processing routines that operate upon it. Investigators of intelligence have, perhaps not surprisingly, focused on the latter.

As the field has developed, however, the objective has deviated from the 'pure' approach of theorising about intelligence *per se, as a cognitive system*, to a tendency merely to view information processing as the elusive explanation of individual differences in test scores that psychometric reasoning has been unable to provide. As Jensen (1987) explained:

According to the information processing view, there are individual differences in the speed or efficiency of the various elementary processes, in the presence or absence of certain metaprocesses, and these differences account for the differences in performance on psychometric tests and the kinds of educational and occupational performance criteria predicted by conventional test scores.

(Jensen 1987: 82)

This turn to information processing as an extension of the aims of IQ testing has led to two main streams of investigation: that which seeks to find, within the information processing of the system, a more objective and direct *measure* of intelligence than is offered in IQ tests; and that which analyses IQ-type tasks in terms of information processing routines for ways in which to *characterise* intelligence. We shall examine these in this chapter. In Chapter 4 we shall examine alternative theories which stress the importance of (among other things) the knowledge base.

The speed of information processing

One prominent recent focus concerns the speed of information processing. This topic, in fact, has a long and curious history. In the nineteenth century mental speed was not thought to be an attribute of intelligence. On the contrary, as Spencer (1855) argued, 'Those having well-developed nervous

systems will display a relatively marked premeditation – an habitual representation of more various possibilities . . . a greater tendency to suspense of
judgement and an easier modification of judgements that have been formed'.

As we saw in Chapter 2, although Galton presupposed that intelligence was
essentially a 'biological' phenomenon (at least in the sense that individual
differences in what was popularly referred to as intelligence were essentially
biological differences) he conceived it in more mechanistic terms, manifested as
mental speed or energy. These, he reasoned, could be tapped by sensory or
physiological measures, rather than psychological ones (even had such measures
been devised). In the former category Galton included measures of reaction
time (RT), or the speed with which subjects responded to given signals, and
these were administered in surveys by Galton in this country and by others
such as Wissler (1901) and J.M. Cattell (Cattell and Ferrand, 1896) in the USA.
The results were considered to be disappointing, however, because they failed
to correlate with subjective impressions of intelligence, such as educational
success, or 'race' or social status. For example Wissler found little association
between such measures and his students' scholastic performance; they were
later discarded as useful measures of intelligence.

It has to be remembered, of course, that Galton was primarily interested in
the utility of such measures in connection with his projected eugenics programmes (mentioned in Chapter 2), and that social class and 'racial' differences
were very much in the air, especially in the USA. Thus when Bache (1895)
administered reaction time tests to Whites and Blacks in the USA he found
Whites to be inferior. This he attributed to the fact that the Whites' 'reactions
were slower because they belonged to a more deliberate and reflective race'.
And Thorndike (1903) concluded that 'the apparent mental attainments of
children of inferior races may be due to lack of inhibition, and so witness
precisely to a deficiency in mental growth'.

Anyway, as we have seen, a different approach to the measure of intelligence –
that of Binet and Simon – was eventually favoured: one based on more global,
albeit more obscure, performances which were selected for their *empirical* rather
than their theoretical relation with school performance. Of course there has been
a long-standing suspicion that this wasn't really intelligence, but some pale
shadow or secondary reflection. Hebb (1949) made a distinction between Intelligence A (the hypothetical biological intelligence that Galton sought); Intelligence B (the manifestation of this in everyday life); and Intelligence C (that
which is expressed as a score on an IQ test). The last decade or so has seen
renewed efforts to measure Intelligence A through what have been called
Galtonian paradigms or measures (Carlson and Widaman 1987). We shall first
simply review these efforts and some of their results before turning to a critique.

Simple and choice reaction time

Most of the recent work on reaction time stems from the work of Hick (1952), who used a simple apparatus that has been used in many investigations since (see Figure 3.1). Basically this involves a 'home' button which a subject keeps depressed until a light appears nearby. 'In front of this is a target button, which the subject must depress as quickly as possible after the light comes on. The time from 'light on' to the time the subject lifts his or her finger from the home button is usually called the reaction time (RT) although it is sometimes called decision time. The time taken to move from the home button to the target button is called the 'movement time' (MT). When there is only one target button (with one light) the former time is called 'simple' reaction time. When these are multiplied so that the subject has to judge direction of movement prior to movement itself, this is called 'choice reaction time'.

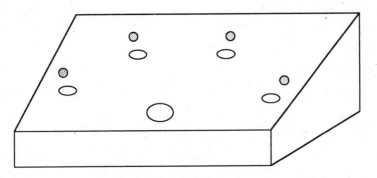

Figure 3.1　Reaction time apparatus (diagrammatic) showing the start button and four choice buttons

Hick (1952) found that RT increased with the number of choices that had to be made, but the slope differed for different individuals (see Figure 3.2). These parameters have formed the basic paradigm with which most of the recent work has been done, although there have been others (see Carlson and Widaman 1987). And it has been assumed that the slope of the RT curve in the multiple-choice reaction time task is not merely one more 'proxy' measure of intelligence like the IQ test, but rather a measure of the quality or efficiency of the fundamental biological 'core' of intelligence (neuro-anatomical structure and function) itself.

How can we know this? The logic of recent investigators, as with those at the turn of the century, is that individual differences on these measures correlate with those on IQ tests, and that the more recent investigations (unlike those earlier measures, mentioned above) do, in fact, display such correlations. This may seem a circular logic in view of the fact that the turn to such measures was motivated in part through dissatisfaction with the IQ tests that are now being used to validate them (a point we shall return to below). But let us look at some of these recent claims.

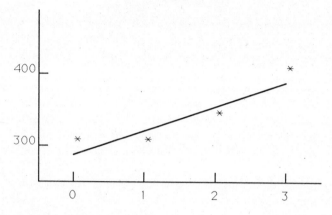

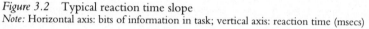

Figure 3.2   Typical reaction time slope
Note: Horizontal axis: bits of information in task; vertical axis: reaction time (msecs)

Correlates of RT performance

Briefly, RT parameters have included median RT; median RT for two, four or eight target buttons; slopes and intercepts of the plots of these; and inter-individual variability of RT. A variety of IQ measures have been used. Moderate correlations have been found between each of these parameters and IQ test scores. For example, Jensen (1982) reports correlations of about −0.40 between slope of RT (i.e. increase in RT with increasing choices) and IQ; and Jensen and Vernon (1986) conclude that the correlation between slope and IQ is −0.30, although not all studies have shown this (Carlson and Widaman 1987). After a series of studies showing similar results, Detterman (1987: 190) concludes, 'there can be little question about the relationship between [RT] and intelligence. The correlation is about −0.30 in the general population.'

Such correlations have been found to be interesting, but not without problems. Longstreth (1984) has found a number of damaging errors in Jensen's methods, reportings and analyses of data, such that the 'evidence' for the RT–IQ relationship 'is, in fact, almost nonexistent'. And as Eysenck (1987) concurs

> Contrary to the expectations expressed by both Jensen and the Erlangen school, neither the Hick slope nor the increase in RT–IQ correlations with increase in the number of bits in the stimulus array can be said to have given very high correlations.

> (Eysenck 1987: 57)

Moreover, the biggest correlation is consistently found between RT *variability* and IQ. (We shall have more to say about this below.) What explanations could there be for the correlations that have been obtained? And why are they so low? Finally what is their theoretical significance?

First, as Detterman (1987) explains, reaction time is itself not as simple a process as it at first seems. It involves a number of complex cognitive and non-cognitive factors. The possible factors cited by Detterman include understand-ing instructions; familiarity with the equipment; motivation in the task; sensory acuity; different strategies in various aspects of response selection and con-struction; and so on. Detterman argues that RT data cannot be understood until the role of such processes has been clarified.

In other words, as with IQ, rather than reaction time presenting a seemingly clear-cut measure, there is still considerable doubt about what differences in performance are actually differences *in*. Moreover, partly as a result of debate generated by such studies, the whole presupposition of 'smart means fast' is again being questioned. As Sternberg (1984) argues, this may be true in some situations, but what is more critical is knowing when to be slow and when to be fast, i.e. *control* of speed according to task demands. The debate has also drawn attention to the diversity of factors that enter into performance dif-ferences on what is supposed to be 'intelligence' pure and simple, whether it be on a reaction time test or an IQ test.

Keating and MacLean (1987) express two kinds of threat to the approach so far. The first concerns the validity of the processing parameters identified: 'there seems to be an emerging pattern within this literature that the more carefully specified and rigorously validated the processing parameters become, the *less* cognitive ability variance they account for' (1987: 266). The second concerns the ambiguous interpretation of the measures or parameters them-selves. 'The major concern is that such parameters may capture more than just processing variance; indeed, they may often be partly or wholly confounded with other, non-processing aspects of performance' (1987: 266). This means that even a simple measure such as reaction time may not be measuring what investigators think it is measuring.

Thus the RT studies show that as the complexity of the task (i.e. the further we get away from the basic processes) increases, the correlation with IQ increases. Even if we were to accept that IQ is a reasonable measure of intel-ligence, this kind of relationship would show that the same intelligence was no simple, single factor like the hypothetical *g* (Detterman 1987). In other words it involves far more than any basic 'neural efficiency'. Carlson and Widaman (1987) have considered the role of attention, arousal and orientation on inter-individual *variability* in RT (the factor which correlates most with IQ). They cite studies using electro-cortical measures, and other studies, indicating that level of arousal and attention does indeed affect RT.

Keating and Maclean (1987) suggest a similar explanation for the RT variability–IQ correlation. Low variability means more consistency, which 'is more easily interpreted as the result of how much voluntary, sustained effort the subjects are willing to put into the tasks' (1987: 255). This raises the possibility that differences in attention and arousal (perhaps affected, in turn, by uncertainty or confidence in the test situation) account for much of the indi-vidual differences in IQ and in RT tasks, and also explains the moderate correlations between these measures. (Meanwhile, of course, we must not lose sight of the fact that IQ appears to have little correlation with real-life tasks anyway.)

Inspection time

Another approach of the 'new' intelligence research has involved investigating 'inspection time' as a correlate of IQ. Since the issues here closely parallel those surrounding reaction time, just discussed, we shall be brief. Inspection time refers to the time taken to distinguish accurately between, say, two lines of different length presented for brief, but slowly increasing, periods on a screen facing the subject. The length of time required for accurate discrimination is considered to be a measure of 'processing speed' (Nettlebeck 1987), and the subject's mean processing speed is compared with an IQ measure.

A number of studies have reported moderate correlations with IQ in both adults and children (Nettlebeck 1987; Nettlebeck and Young 1989). Although these results have been questioned on a variety of methodological grounds (e.g. Mackintosh 1986; Howe 1988), a correlation in the range of 0.3–0.5 seems a possibility. The question is, once again, what are we to make of this? On the one hand we don't know what differences in either of these measures are really differences *in*; and we have no idea what explains the correlation, if it exists. As Stough and Nettlebeck (1989: 374) concur, 'these correlations do not provide us with any explanation for the underlying factors mediating this association'. As with RT, a wide range of non-cognitive variables, such as attention, confidence, motivation, and so on, could be responsible.

Electro-encephalograms, evoked potentials and IQ

The 'reading' of electrical activity of 'the brain' from electrodes placed at various places on the scalp started in the first half of this century. The pattern of such activity came to be called the electro-encephalogram (EEG), and the fact that the pattern changed with mental activity led to the belief that the EEG could reveal much about the 'inner' or physiological basis of intelligence.

Between the 1930s and the 1960s much effort was expended in demonstrating correlations between aspects of the EEG and IQ test performance, with mixed claims and counterclaims (see Giannitrapani 1985 for a brief history). The upshot of these studies is, as Stein (1982) explains, 'apart from a few situations, such as sleep, cortical damage and epilepsy, the EEG has proved rather disappointing. For more subtle analyses of cerebral activities, the EEG is a crude tool' (1982: 308). Most recent work has been concerned with the effects of perceptual stimulation on aspects of the EEG, which are amplified by averaging with computers. We shall now describe the use of these average evoked potentials.

Averaged evoked potentials (AEPs)

The presentation of a light flash or an audible click evokes a wave of electrical activity in the EEG that is superimposed on the background EEG activity. The 'fuzziness' of this 'evoked potential' precludes any direct analysis, however, without averaging similar responses over many repetitions of the stimulus. The process is described by Stein (1982):

> With modern computers, the electrical activity evoked by the light can be detected through the head, even though it is attenuated 100-fold by the short-circuiting effect of the c.s.f. [cerebro-spinal fluid between the membranes surrounding the brain], dura, skull and scalp. Since only the potential evoked by a stimulus is locked in time with it, whilst other fluctuations of the EEG occur randomly, a computer may be used to sum together EEG potentials at equal time intervals following repeated presentations of the stimulus. The size of the potential evoked by the stimulus is thus increased many times, whereas the background EEG, not being related in time to the stimulus, tends to cancel out completely. The advantage of this averaging process over simply amplifying EEG voltages following a stimulus is that only the signal which is of interest is enhanced, whilst background EEG is reduced. In communications jargon, the 'signal-to-noise ratio' is increased – in fact by the square root of the number of recordings averaged.
>
> (Stein 1982: 308)

A number of early studies using this technique (e.g. Weinberg 1969; Ertl and Schafer 1969) were considered interesting, but not revealing. The study most commonly cited is that of Blinkhorn and Hendrickson (1982). These authors measured the 'complexity' or unevenness of the AEP waveform by running a length of string along the trace, and arriving at a 'string-length': the more complex the waveform, the greater the string-length. They found that, across a group of adult subjects, this string-length correlated with Raven's IQ to a value of 0.54. Elsewhere, D.E. Hendrickson (1982) has reported a correlation of 0.72 between such a measure and performance on the WAIS, a value which Eysenck (1986: 19) describes as a 'truly astounding result', suggesting that 'to a very large extent, both sets of scores measure an identical *g*' (1986: 21). Substantial correlations have also been reported in other similar studies (e.g. Schafer 1982; 1984; Haier *et al.* 1983).

Criticisms of EEG and AEPs

Do such studies and their results help us build a convincing and testable theory of intelligence, that might in turn be converted into accepted scientific knowledge? Some psychologists think so. For example Eysenck (1987) thinks that we have such a theory:

we may equate Intelligence A (biological intelligence) with some such concept as error-free transmission of information through the cortex. . . . Differences in error-free transmission lead to differences in IQ, mainly through the influence of error-free transmission on mental speed.

(Eysenck 1987: 58)

In consequence, 'we are faced with a revolution in the theory and measurement of intelligence' (1987: 58). Elsewhere he argues, 'we have come quite close to the physiological measurement of the genotype underlying the phenotypic IQ test results on which we have had to rely so far' (Eysenck 1982: 6). Likewise Carlson and Widaman (1987) argue that 'the recent research on early evoked potentials is astounding in its implications' (1987: 78).

Is there anything of substance behind such hyperbole? First, let us look at the reliability of the results themselves. Mackintosh (1986) has revealed several problems in this respect. For example the Hendrickson (1982) sample consisted of four different groups, only one of which yielded significant AEP–IQ correlations. One of these was a group of people living in an institution for the severely subnormal, who produced some of the longest string measures of all. So the picture from these data is hardly complete and consistent. Similarly the Haier *et al.* (1983) 'replication' consisted of twelve correlations between IQ and various string-length measures, only three of which were statistically significant. Mackintosh (1986) himself reports further attempts to replicate such results without success. In a similar review, Howe (1988: 541) notes that 'Studies published in refereed journals have produced virtually no replicable findings of correlations averaging more than around 0.3 between intelligence test scores and measures of evoked potentials or any other indication of events at the physiological level'.

Second, there is considerable uncertainty about what electrical patterns actually reflect in the nervous system. Giannitrapani (1985: 4) notes that 'The theory that EEG is attributable to gross synchronisation of synaptic potentials and to circulation of impulses in closed self-reexciting chains, articulated by Eccles (1951), has not been replaced by a more viable alternative'. But this doesn't mean very much in terms of specific functions. In what sense could these hard-to-discern and hard-to-interpret patterns be 'physiological intelligence'? Eysenck (1986) tries hard to make some connection by suggesting that the AEP reflects error-free transmission of impulses, and the 'neutral-integrity' of nervous systems such that 'it will be practically impossible for individuals of low neural integrity to maintain long sequences of information-carrying pulse trains' (1986: 18). This suggestion conjures up visions of unruly nerve impulses flying around the system with wide variations in accuracy and state of control, which makes one wonder how the vast majority of humans manage even to *walk* without falling over, let alone produce long sequences of finely articulated actions in everyday activities like talking.

Third, there are the technical problems entailed in gathering evoked potential (EP) data. As Stein (1982: 309) notes, 'the problems of recording from large numbers of neurons simultaneously . . . namely the unknown geometric relations between electrode and neurones and the number of different neurones contributing to the voltage fluctuation – make interpretation of EPs extremely difficult'. Such problems are compounded by the need to average readings elicited by repeated stimulation, 'activity which is known to change with each repetition' (Giannitrapani 1985: 12). The latter notes how the state of attention or arousal has been shown to affect the EP patterns strongly. Poor arousal or attention would tend to produce highly variable patterns which would be 'smoothed-out' by the averaging process, resulting in shorter string-lengths. So, as Mackintosh (1986) points out, the AEP-IQ correlations may simply 'reflect the stability and uniformity of the subject's response over 100 trials of listening to a 30 ms tone' (1986: 11).

In a similar review, Carlson and Widaman (1987) conclude that

> interpretation of the meaning of the early waveforms observed by the Hendricksons, Schafer and others is complicated by several factors: (a) that exogenous factors may be significantly involved in their manifestation; (b) that elective auditory attention may be an important factor in the results . . . ; (c) that meaningful, correct results of cognition may have little to do with average evoked potentials.
>
> (Carlson and Widaman 1987: 78)

So again (as with the RT studies) we have the prospect thrown up that much of the variability in these 'basic' measures and IQ is a reflection of arousal, attention or some other 'orientation' factors, which in turn may arise from a variety of personal and social factors (some of which we shall discuss in Chapter 4).

Componential approaches

The componential approach, again, is based on certain presuppositions about what intelligence is constituted of and how it is best described. It accepts (like every other view described so far) that the popular view of a 'ladder' of intelligence is a legitimate one, but suggests that these differences are situated in performances on coherent tasks rather than some basic, pervasive, single process like mental speed. A component in this sense is a distinct mental operation. 'A component is an elementary information process that operates on internal representations of objects or symbols' (Sternberg 1985b: 59).

The componential approach has become popular only in the 1980s, largely through the work of R.J. Sternberg, so there is still considerable uncertainty about the nature, number and variety of components. Some are thought to be 'affected by learning', for example; while others are thought to be modifiable 'only through medical interventions' (Baron 1985: 365). A typical componential operation, as seen by Sternberg, would include translating a sensory input into a conceptual representation; transforming one conceptual representation into another; or translating a conceptual representation into a motor outut. A component is defined, however, by a level of analysis convenient to an investigator, rather than by some absolute existence (Sternberg 1984a: 281).

Note that components of intelligence in this approach are different from the 'factors' of factor analysis. The latter are statistical distillations of scoring patterns, although they have sometimes been thought of (or reified) as subprocesses of intelligence in a similar sense. Such a straightforward translation is a mistake, however.

A number of different theories of components have been proposed, and since the business is still highly speculative, these have varied enormously. In one review, Sternberg (1985b) instances Carroll's theory, which posits ten types of components; and Brown's theory, which proposes two *categories* of processes, each of which contains many components. Sternberg (1984; 1985a) has himself proposed a componential theory made up of three kinds of 'knowledge acquisition' components, three kinds of 'performance components', and ten kinds of 'metacomponents'. The latter are 'decision' or executive processes involved in, for example, selection of particular performance components, or the representations on which they may operate. Examples of performance components include the encoding of stimuli or combination or comparison of stimuli; examples of knowledge-acquisition components (processes used in gaining new knowledge) include the selective encoding and selective comparison of stimuli.

The basic strategy of the componential approach is only partly a direct exposition of the components themselves (and through them, of the nature of intelligence); another is to explore how these different components are related to individual differences in test performances (usually IQ test performances). In this way individual differences on overall task performances may be reduced to differences on some particular aspect or component of the task. 'The basic idea is that components represent latent abilities of some kind that give rise to individual differences in measured intelligence and in real-world performance' (Sternberg 1985b: 225). In reality this strategy has reduced to seeking correlations between parameters of components on the one hand and test scores on the other.

A good illustration of this approach is that of research into 'analogical reasoning': in fact the kind of item very common in IQ tests, as indicated in Chapter 2. These items usually take the form 'A is to B as C is to –' (with various options for 'D' presented for selection). The research has entailed breaking the subjects' behaviour down, impressionistically, into various steps (the putative components) and comparing these across individuals with respect to overall performance. In this way, several sub-stages in the overall process have been identified (Sternberg 1977; Sternberg and Rifkin 1979; for review see Pellegrino 1985):

1 *encoding*, or the representation of the salient attributes of the stimulus in memory
2 *inference* of the changes in A necessary to produce B
3 *mapping* the correspondence between A and C •
4 *applying* the changes inferred in 2 to C to produce the 'best' D
5 *evaluation/justification* of the selection
6 *response*.

The role of each of these steps or components has been explored by breaking the tasks down in order first, to isolate the time spent, and accuracies obtained, in each of these steps, and second, to assess the effects, on each of these times and accuracies, of various manipulations such as varying the number of elements to be encoded, varying the number of transformations involved, and so on. The contribution of these various components to overall performance is then examined.

In this way, times and accuracies on the different components may be compared with IQ score; or the performances of high and low IQ individuals may be compared with respect to these components. Thus it has been found, for example, that individuals who perform well on such items in a test tend to spend *longer* in the encoding component than do those who perform less well on such items. The opposite has been found for most other components (Sternberg 1977; Pellegrino 1985), and correlations between latencies on these and reference test scores typically range from 0.4 to 0.8 (Sternberg and Gardner 1983). As with all such studies the time spent on 'encoding' is taken to reflect a specific cognitive operation or component, the relative efficiency of which is taken to be causal to intelligence.

Another illustration of the approach is that of Carpenter and Just (1986), who monitored subjects' eye-movements to infer processes underlying solution to Cube Comparison tasks like that shown in Figure 3.3. Several differences were observed between those who tended to perform well on such items and those who performed less well, as assessed by a battery of psychometric tasks. Thus 'high spatial' subjects tended to rotate mentally around a diagonal axis, whereas 'low spatial' subjects tended to rotate in steps around the edges. Also the latter tended to execute a given rotation more than once in a trial, which added to the total time of execution. A further difference

was that the low spatials had extreme difficulty keeping track of information that was not 'visible' in their image. Their error rates soared whenever a letter went to a 'hidden' side and was supposed to reappear after a second rotation. Low spatials couldn't or didn't keep track of letters that were rotated out of their mind's eye.

(Carpenter and Just 1986: 235)

Studies which have concentrated on accuracy rather than latency of response have shown parallel results. Less accurate individuals (including

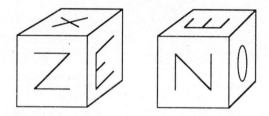

Figure 3.3   Could these be the same cube? The cube comparison task
Source: Modified from Carpenter and Just 1986

children relative to adults) fail to perform the *inference* and *application* components so readily, and tend to be more easily distracted. Pellegrino (1985) provides a review of studies involving series completion, another kind of common IQ test item.

Criticisms of the componential approach

Perhaps the first criticism of the approach is that it reduces intelligence to sequences of routines or quasi-mechanical operations which are distinct from the knowledge base on which they operate, i.e. it is excessively mechanical. As Gardner (1984: 23) commented on the approach in general, 'Throughout, one encounters the healthy, if somewhat unexamined, American emphasis on mechanics: on what is done, in what order, by what mechanism, in order to yield a particular effect or result'. But the approach, he argues, 'lacks an articulated theory', so that 'it foreshadows certain long-term problems'.

One effect of this mechanical conception is to over-simplify the explanatory logic. Thus Sternberg (1985a) identifies only three interesting parameters of intelligence components: the duration of execution; the probability of execution; and the probability of being executed correctly. By implication, all the interesting properties of human intelligence in general, and of individuals in particular, are described by specifying values on these parameters. Accordingly people are said to vary (for unspecified reasons in Sternberg's theory) in the efficiency or power of these mechanical processes; and these differences in turn are thought to 'explain' differences in IQ (which are usually assumed to approximate differences in intelligence).

This is not the only scientific strategy in a field such as this. A more 'organic' approach might see mental operations as part and parcel of the stored representations of the world, i.e. of the 'structure' of our concepts, and so on (Richardson 1987; Richardson and Carthy 1989). Different representations mean different functions in much the way that the functions of the tissues of the liver or kidney are inseparable from their structures. The appearance of 'latent abilities' may be more a function of the specific tasks than of the cognitive system as such.

The componential approach has certainly been heuristic in terms of hypothesis generation and testing; but there are obvious limits to the notion that all our mental processes consist of independent, sequential operations acting on a 'switch-on'/'switch-off' basis. Thus identification of components achieves only an idealistic description of tasks that have to be done mentally, without in any sense indicating whether or how they *are* done mentally. In such situations there is always a danger of reification. It is important not to confuse readily observable, or otherwise apparent, sub-stages in the execution of a task with the internal processes by which that execution is brought about. These may be quite different operations. Sternberg (1984) asks us to consider the component 'mapping' involved in analogies like LAWYER is to CLIENT as DOCTOR is to (a) PATIENT, (b) MEDICINE. 'Mapping calls for the discovery of the higher-order relation between the first and second halves of the analogy' (1984: 281). But giving this 'discovering' a name doesn't tell us how the 'intelligence' at work achieves it.

Richardson (1986) argues that this kind of reasoning smacks of the nominal fallacy – that naming something is the same thing as identifying it – i.e. a 'componential fallacy'. In a similar vein Butterfield (1986) argues that the approach of Sternberg and others is *ad hoc*, in that it, in spite of implying mechanisms behind the components, neither these, nor the relations between them, are specified. As with other information-processing accounts of cognition, based on flow-charts and boxes, 'each box specifies a function without saying how it is to be accomplished (one says in effect: put a little man in there to do the job)' (Dennett 1978, quoted by Palmer 1987: 59). No doubt this largely *ad hoc*, intuitive approach explains the proliferation of diverse components in different accounts by different authors. The approach, moreover, tends to set aside awkward questions about how the components (including meta-components) themselves are organised and implemented, as if this had nothing to do with intelligence.

Of course it can be argued that conjectures of this sort, and the analytic breakdown of tasks, are an important first step in any theory-construction, and this is quite true. Components or factors are conceived inductively for their potential explanatory value; but we must not impute strong explanatory power to them before a coherent theory exists, and has been properly tested. This tendency does seem to exist. For example, Sternberg (1985a) reports that individuals vary in the time taken to complete each of the steps he calls components, and that the differences correlate with scores on IQ tests. The logic described above is then applied to reach the conclusion that not only are the components 'real', but also they explain differences in performance on IQ-type tasks, namely 'different levels of power in the execution of the various kinds of components' (Sternberg 1984: 308). Readers will by now be aware that there are many possible explanations for such correlations, other than the existence of cognitive processing, in fixed components varying in power or efficiency.

In fact an important criticism is that performances on individual components do not, in any case, correlate highly with criterion measures, whether of psychometric test scores, or other 'real-life' criteria (for example Eghan 1978 found no relation between rotation performance on tasks like the cube comparisons, illustrated above, and performance on aircraft pilot training). The higher correlations usually quoted refer to some combinations of component performance, such as encoding and application *together*, or justification and response *together* (Sternberg and Gardner 1983; Detterman 1984).

Another criticism – stemming again from the mechanistic nature of componential theory – is that componential analysis works best on simple, easily specified tasks that are almost exclusively IQ test items (Keating and MacLean 1986). Are everyday, real-life manifestations of intelligence analysable in such terms (again bearing in mind that IQ performance seems to be unrelated to such intelligence anyway)?

In response to such problems Sternberg (1985b) himself admits that the identification of components alone will not give an adequate account of the nature of intelligence. Partly because of this Sternberg (1985a) has implicated 'higher' strategy components, or metacomponents, and suggested that this is where individual differences in intelligence primarily lie. But this leaves the awkward question of what controls the metacomponents or 'central executive', and how? Hasn't that got something to do with intelligence?

Multiple intelligences

Another theory that looks for cognitive grounding of intelligence – although eschewing the mechanistic nature of componential theories – is Gardner's (1984) theory of 'multiple intelligence'. The basic presupposition is the existence within the cognitive/neurobiological system of discrete information-processing operations or mechanisms which deal with the specific, but different, kinds of information which humans encounter in the course of their regular activities.

> One might go so far as to define a human intelligence as a neural mechanism or computational system which is genetically programmed to be activated or 'triggered' by certain kinds of internally or externally presented information. Examples would include sensitivity to pitch relations as one core of musical intelligence, or the ability to imitate movement by others as one core of bodily intelligence.
>
> (Gardner 1984: 64)

Among these different 'modules' Gardner includes linguistic intelligence; musical intelligence; logico-mathematical intelligence; spatial intelligence; bodily kinaesthetic intelligence; and personal intelligences (access to personal feelings, relations with others, and so on). The operations of which they are constituted are conceived to be essentially genetically pre-programmed, although subject to some developmental flexibility (and thus amenable to

cultural specialisation and to educational assistance). As grounds for these conjectures, Gardner includes a wide range of considerations such as the organisation of the nervous system, the consequences of brain damage, the existence of
individuals exceptional in a particular 'intelligence'; and many others. The
theory has already suggested some practical applications in schools (e.g.
Gardner 1989), although the results of these are still to be properly evaluated.

There are a number of possible criticisms of such a theory, and Gardner
himself (1984) acknowledges and discusses some of these. One of them is that
the theory is rather vague (though no more so than other theories) in that the
way that intelligence emerges from 'dumb', innate, computational processes is
not specified. Another problem – one which relates to all theories of pre-
programmed 'constraints' on learning and development – is that it implies
some stable conditions of evolution and natural selection at some time in the
past. As Gardner notes, these intelligences are 'eventually mobilized in the
service of diverse social roles and functions' (1984: 278). But many have argued
that it was precisely the rapid *changeability* of human circumstances, especially
that of social roles and functions, that is responsible for the highly adaptable
human intelligence we have (Holloway 1975). Pre-programmed constraints
would be a great handicap to such adaptability (Richardson 1988).

Finally, we have to note the dangers of reification once again. As Gardner
(1984: 63) admits, 'The selection (or rejection) of a candidate intelligence is
reminiscent more of an artistic judgement than of a scientific assessment. Bor-
rowing a concept from statistics, one might think of the procedure as a kind of
"subjective" factor analysis'. As we saw in Chapter 2, the bold conjecturing of
such 'factors' may be useful starting hypotheses which must not be taken too
seriously until the experimental work they dictate has actually been carried out
(and rival interpretations of the same data resolved). Gardner (e.g. 1989) continues to develop his theory in this way and needs to be watched with interest.

General criticisms of the information-processing approach

There are many more general criticisms of the information-processing approach to intelligence. Some relate to cognitive studies in general; others relate
to their specific application in this particular area. We shall consider these first.

At the beginning of this chapter we noted the scientifically superior logic
of the process-oriented approach as an approach to understanding intelligence, because the logic encourages hypthetico-deductive testing of empirically constructed *theory* rather than merely confirming an informal hunch
or model, or projecting inductive constructions from test scores or other
observations. As Keating and MacLean (1987) explain with respect to componential approaches

> rather than relying on *post hoc* interpretations of empirically derived fac-
> tors, componential analysis permits [we would contend that it requires]

some level of *a priori* theorising about how the proposed processes in fact
relate systematically to the complex cognitive skill or ability.

(Keating and MacLean 1987: 248)

Unfortunately this 'systematically relating' does not seem to have happened
very much. As we have seen, the essential scientific tool of most process-
oriented studies so far has been the correlation coefficient – coupled with a
conspicuous haste to conclude (on the basis of correlations) that this or that
process is what intelligence 'really' is. In other words the logic seems to have
gone awry.

Perhaps the most conspicuous symptom of this is that, whereas the resort to
the process-oriented approach was avowedly to break out of the 'atheoretic'
IQ approach, it is strange to find validation of processes and components, and
their new measures, being sought solely in correlations with IQ test performance (Estes 1986). This is the same old circular logic that we were supposed
to be escaping. Thus Sternberg (1984a) speaks of the need to

> escape from the vicious circularity that has confronted much past research
> on intelligence, in which . . . new conceptions are then validated (or
> invalidated!) against the old conceptions for lack of any better external
> criteria. There is need to generate some kind of external standard that
> goes beyond the view, often subtly hidden, that intelligence is what IQ
> tests happen to measure. For, whatever its operational appeal, this view
> lacks substantive theoretical grounding, and when IQ test scores are used
> as the 'external' criterion against which new theories and tests are vali-
> dated, one is essentially accepting this operational view.
>
> (Sternberg 1984a: 270)

Yet Sternberg is just as willing to adopt a test-centred view when he argues, on
the basis of test scores, that 'Almost all children will eventually walk . . . but
not all children become, say, adept analogical reasoners or spatial visualisers'
(1988: 286). Why has this trap prevailed?

One reason may be that the ontological commitment, or world view, underlying the 'new' approaches is unchanged: the new approaches are simply
being used to attempt to vindicate the same presuppositions of strength, power,
energy, etc., as the old IQ approach. Thus Eysenck (1987) continues to see
these 'processes' in terms of some all-pervasive level of cerebral energy. And as
Jensen (1987) explains:

> The as yet unrealised task of information processing research is to show
> that individual differences in the same limited number of elementary
> cognitive processes are indeed involved in a wide variety of superfically
> different kinds of test items and can thereby afford an adequate explana-
> tion of the sources of variation in, and correlations between, standard
> psychometric tests.
>
> (Jensen 1987: 82)

And although he speaks of the need to see intelligence *in context*, Sternberg (1984a: 308), as we have already seen, readily alludes to 'different levels of power in the execution of various kinds of components', as the best description of the manifestation of intelligence.

The approach appears to be dominated, in other words, by utilitarian or pragmatic objectives. This was noted by Montangero (1985) in comparing Piaget's theory (see Chapter 5) with that of the 'cognitive' psychologists:

> Since the aim of current [i.e. cognitive] approaches is to seize the functioning of thought, they study how the mind works when facing specific problems. . . . This particularity as well as the everlasting tendency to define intelligence by the tasks achieved rather than by its structural or procedural characteristics is in accordance with the pragmatic character of the American mind. In the United States psychology tends to focus on what is useful and efficient. It is why it looks for operational constructs rather than for comprehensive theories. This lack of more or less general theories renders more evident an important feature of current approaches . . . their fragmentary character.
>
> (Montangero 1985: 98–9)

Of course it is possible to cite a variety of other specific problems in this approach. One is the conspicuous lack of precision in talking about the processes themselves. As mentioned above, 'mental energy' or 'neural efficiency' can mean a variety of things, and can be interpreted in a positive or negative light according to the argument we want to bolster. A similar lack of precision emerges in the use of the term 'intelligence' (in reality, nearly always some form of IQ) of which the 'processes' are supposed to be the neurobiological base. Thus even the briefest scan of the literature reveals a motley collection including the Raven's Progressive Matrices (e.g. Blinkhorn and Hendrickson 1982); Wechsler Adult Intelligence Scale (Hendrickson 1982); the California Test of Basic Skills (Carlson and Widaman 1987); the Woodcock–Johnson Psycho-educational Battery (Horn 1987); the McCarthy Scales of Children's Abilities (Horn 1987); and many others. Such lack of precision in terms and measures is not conducive to clear theory-construction and theory-testing.

Indeed it seems to make the slipperiness of the idea of intelligence all the more apparent. There appears to be a general feeling that the information-processing approaches are at last getting us down to the cognitive or biological 'nitty-gritty' of intelligence. Yet occasionally we are warned that intelligence is not a 'thing' but a concept. For example, in spite of attempting to describe cognitive components of intelligence, Sternberg (1984b) warns that intelligence is merely a social label:

> I would conclude by stressing that whereas cognitive and motivational processes are *discovered*, intelligence is *invented* . . . 'intelligence' is a convenient label for that collection of dispositions that in combination result

in adaptive behaviour in certain social-cultural milieu. It is not any one thing. . . . Rather it is a complex mixture of ingredients. . . . The invention is a societal one.

(Sternberg 1984b: 31, italics in original)

This would surely suggest that the locus of understanding of this concept lies, not in internal information-processing at all, but in the *social* forces which invent it.

One caution which must be made concerns the tendency, in much of contemporary psychology, to turn to 'information processing' or 'cognitive' approaches as a kind of panacea for persistent problems. There appears to be the same lack of substantive theory in cognitive theory in general as there is in its application to an area like intelligence in particular. One salient criticism here concerns the term 'information'. In spite of allusions to 'information processing' the 'information' that is said to be processed is rarely specified with any precision.

This kind of point has been made by several people about the processing approach. Thus in a discussion of the information-processing approach, Newell (1973, quoted by Beilin 1983) noted how each investigation resulted in a unique model for the task, because of lack of clear theory. Newell then went on:

> Our task in psychology is first to discover that structure which is fixed and invariant so that we can theoretically infer the method [used to perform the task] . . . without such a framework within which to work, the generation of new methods, hence new explanations, for old phenomena, will go on ad nauseum. There will be no discipline for it, as there is none now.

(Beilin 1983: 19)

As Beilin (1983) concludes from such discussion

> it would not be amiss to say that information-processing theory, even at this date, is a collection of models lacking a coherent theory of the logical or natural processes by which cognitive structures as wholistic entities are formed.

(Beilin 1983: 19)

Similarly after a review of research in the area, Verster (1987): asks:

> what then is really known about human cognition and intelligence? The only fair answer, shared undoubtedly by most prominent researchers in the field, would seem to be that very little, indeed, is *known*.

(Verster 1987: 96–7, italics in original)

It perhaps seems rather naive to expect to discover the cognitive bases of intelligence, when we know so little about cognition itself. In fact, as we have seen above, the only coherent theory binding most aspirants of the processing approach to intelligence is the strength or 'power' model of intelligence that dominates the psychometric (IQ) approach. The pursuit of the identification of this fundamental 'power' may, as now, be put on different agendas or different maps, but the commitment to the affirmation of an intuitive model of intelligence appears to be the same. The attempt to rescue a disappointing and prescientific notion of intelligence, by propping it up with the seemingly 'harder' concepts of information-processing and cognition is, however, unlikely to succeed, for the reasons just given.

This raises a most important issue. Since it is now being claimed that the understanding of intelligence lies in cognition, would it not be better to devote all our research efforts to the understanding of cognition first? Would not this approach be more fruitful than simply trying to find *ad hoc*, and inevitably vague, cognitive structures to fit our preconceived intelligence? Opinions are likely to differ on this. It may be, as Verster (1987: 99) suggests, 'that a start has been made towards the inevitable merger of psychometric and psychonomic cognitive research' and that, in the mean time, 'researchers should retain full freedom in their approach'. Or it may be, as Newell, Beilin (quoted above) and others have pointed out, that researchers will need to adopt a far more disciplined approach if a respectable and agreeable theory of cognition, and therefore of intelligence, is to be arrived at.

References

Bache, P.M. (1895). Reaction time with reference to race. *Psychological Review*, 2: 474–86.

Baron, J. (1985). What kinds of intelligence components are fundamental? in S.F. Chipman, J.W. Segal and R. Glaser (eds) *Thinking and Learning Skills, Vol. 2: Research and Open Questions*. Hillsdale, NJ, Erlbaum.

Beilin, H. (1983). The new functionalism and Piaget's program. In E.F. Scholnik (ed.) *New Trends in Conceptual Representation: Challenges to Piaget's Theory?* Hillsdale, NJ, Erlbaum.

Blinkhorn, S.F. and Hendrickson, D.E. (1982). Average evoked responses and psychometric intelligence. *Nature*, 295, 596–7.

Butterfield, E.C. (1986). Comments. In Detterman, D.K. and Sternberg, R.J. (eds) *What is Intelligence? Contemporary Viewpoints on its Nature and Definition*. Norwood, NJ, Ablex.

Carlson, J.S. and Widaman, K.F. (1987). Elementary cognitive correlates of *g*: progress and prospects. In P.A. Vernon (ed.) *Speed of Information Processing and Intelligence*. New York, Ablex.

Carpenter, P.A. and Just, M.A. (1986). Spatial ability: an information processing approach to psychometrics. In R.J. Sternberg (ed.) Advances in the Psychology of Human Intelligence, Vol. 3. Hillsdale, NJ, Lawrence Erlbaum.

Casey, G. and Moran, A. (1989). The computational metaphor and cognitive psychology. *Irish Journal of Psychology*, 10: 143–61.

Cattell, J. McK and Ferrand, L. (1896). Physical and mental measurements of the students of Columbia University. *Psychological Review*, 3: 618–48.

Dennett, D. (1978). *Brainstorms*. Montgomery, Bradford Books.

Detterman, D.K. (1984). Understanding cognitive components before postulating metacomponents. *Behavioral and Brain Sciences*, 7: 289–90.

—— (1987). What does reaction time tell us about intelligence. In P.A. Vernon (ed.) *Speed of Information Processing and Intelligence*. New York, Ablex.

Eccles, J.C. (1951). Interpretation of action potentials evoked in the cerebral cortex. *Electroencepholography and Clinical Neurophysiology*, 3: 449–64.

Eghan, D.E. (19788). *Characterising Spatial Ability: Different Mental Processes Reflected in Accuracy and Latency Scores*. Murray Hill, NJ, Bell Laboratories.

Ertl, J. and Schafer, E. (1969). Brain response correlates of psychometric intelligence. *Nature*, 223: 421–2.

Estes, W.K. (1986). Where is intelligence? Detterman, D.K. and Sternberg, R.J. (eds) (1986). *What is Intelligence? Contemporary Viewpoints on its Nature and Definition*. Norwood, NJ, Ablex.

Eysenck, H.J. (1982). *A Model for Intelligence*. New York, Springer.

—— (1984). Intelligence versus behaviour. *Behavioral and Brain Sciences*, 7: 290–1.

—— (1986). The theory of intelligence and the psychophysiology of cognition. In R.J. Sternberg (ed.) *Advances in the Psychology of Human Intelligence*, Vol. 3. Hillsdale, NJ, Erlbaum.

—— (1987). Speed of information processing, reaction time, and the theory of intelligence. in P.A. Vernon (ed.) *Speed of Information Processing and Inteligence*. New York, Ablex.

Gardner, H. (1984). *Frames of Mind: The Theory of Multiple Intelligences*. London, Heinemann.

—— (1989). Project Zero: an introduction to Arts Propel. *Journal of Art and Design Education*, 8: 167–81.

Giannitrapani, D. (1985). *The Electrophysiology of Intellectual Functions*, Basel, Karger.

Haier, R.J., Robinson, D.L., Braden, W. and Williams, D. (1983). Electrical potentials of the cerebral cortex and psychometric intelligence. *Personality and Individual Differences*, 4: 591–9.

Hebb, D.O. (1949). *The Organisation of Behaviour*. New York, Wiley.

Hendrickson, D.E. (1982). The biological basis of intelligence. In H.J. Eysenck (ed.) *A Model for Intelligence*. New York, Springer Verlag.

Hick, W. (1952). On the rate of gain of information. *Quarterly Journal of Experimental Psychology*, 4: 11–26.

Holloway, R.L. (1975). *The Role of Human Social Behavior in the Evolution of the Brain*. New York, American Museum of Natural History.

Horn, J. (1986). Intellectual ability concepts. In R.J. Sternberg (ed.) *Advances in the Psychology of Human Intelligence*, vol. 3. Hillsdale, NJ, Erlbaum.

—— (1987). A context for understanding information processing studies of human abilities. In P.A. Vernon (ed.) *Speed of Information Processing and Intelligence*. New York, Ablex.

Howe, M.J.A. (1988). The hazards of using correlational evidence as a means of identifying the causes of individual ability differences: a rejoinder to Sternberg and a reply to Miles. *British Journal of Psychology*, 79: 539–45.

Jensen, A.R. (1982). Reaction time and psychometric *g*. In H.J. Eysenck (ed.) *A Model for Intelligence*. Berlin, Springer-Verlag.

—— (1987). Individual differences in mental ability. In J.A. Glover and R.R. Ronning (eds) *Historical Foundations of Educational Psychology*. New York, Plenum Press.

Jensen, A.R. and Vernon, P.A. (1986). Jensen's reaction-time studies: a reply to Longstreth. *Intelligence*, 10: 153–79.

Kail, R. and Pellegrino, J.W. (1985). *Human Intelligence: Perspectives and Prospects*. New York, Freeman.

Keating, D.P. and MacLean, D.J. (1987). Cognitive processing, cognitive ability, and development: a reconsideration. In P.A. Vernon (ed.) *Speed of Information Processing and Intelligence*. New York, Ablex.

Longstreth, L.E. (1984). Jensen's reaction-time investigations of intelligence: a critique. *Intelligence*, 8: 139–60.

Mackintosh, N.J. (1986). The biology of intelligence? *British Journal of Intelligence*, 77: 1–18.

Marr, D.B. and Sternberg, R.J. (1987). The role of mental speed in intelligence: a triarchic perspective. In P.A. Vernon (ed.) *Speed of Information Processing and Intelligence*. New York, Ablex.

Montangero, J. (1985). *Genetic Epistemology: Yesterday and Today*. New York, The Graduate School and Univesity Centre.

Nettlebeck, T. (1987). Inspection time and intelligence. In P.A. Vernon (ed.) *Speed of Information Processing and Intelligence*. New York, Ablex.

Nettlebeck, T. and Young, R. (1989). Inspection time and intelligence in 6-year-old children. *Personality and Individual Differences*, 10: 605–14.

Newell, A. (1973). You can't play 20 questions with nature and win: projective comments on the papers of this symposium. In W.G. Chase (ed.) *Visual Information Processing*. New York, Academic Press.

Palmer, A. (1987). Cognitivism and computer simulation. In A. Costall and A. Still (eds) *Cognitive Psychology in Question*. New York, St Martin's Press.

Pellegrino, J.W. (1985). Inductive reasoning ability. In R.J. Sternberg (ed.) *Human Abilities: An Information Processing Approach*. New York, Freeman.

Richardson, K. (1986). Intelligence theory? Or tools for social selection? *Behavioral and Brain Sciences*, 9: 579–81.

—— (1987). The abstraction of relations versus the abstraction of independent cues in concept formation. *British Journal of Psychology*, 78: 519–44.

—— (1988). *Understanding Psychology*. Milton Keynes, Open University Press.

Richardson, K. and Carthy, T. (1989). Concept structures and concept functions: inference from incomplete information. *Acta Psychologica*, 72: 81–102.

Schafer, E.W.P. (1982). Neural adaptability: a biological determinant of behavioural intelligence. *International Journal of Neuroscience*, 17: 183–91.

—— (1984). Habituation of evoked cortical potential correlates with intelligence. *Psychophysiology*, 21: 597.

Spencer, H. (1855). *Principles of Psychology*. London, Williams Norgate.

Stein, J.F. (1982). *Introduction to Neurophysiology*. Oxford, Blackwell.

Sternberg, R.J. (1977). *Intelligence, Information Processing, and Analogical Reasoning: The Componential Analysis of Human Abilities*. Hillsdale, NJ, Erlbaum.

—— (1984a). Toward a triarchic theory of human intelligence. *Behavioral and Brain Sciences*, 7: 269–315.

—— (1984b). A contextualist view of the nature of intelligence. In P. Fry (ed.) *Changing Conceptions of Intelligence and Intellectual Functioning: Current Theory and Research.* Amsterdam, North-Holland.

—— (1985a). *Beyond IQ: A Triarchic Theory of Human Intelligence.* Cambridge, Cambridge University Press.

—— (1985b). Instrumental and componential approaches to the nature and training of intelligence. In S.F. Chipman, J.W. Segal and R. Glaser (eds) *Thinking and Learning Skills*, vol. 2, *Research and Open Questions.* Hillsdale, NJ, Erlbaum.

—— (1986). Introduction. In R.J. Sternberg (ed.) *Advances in the Psychology of Human Intelligence*, Vol. 3, Hillsdale, NJ, Lawrence Erlbaum.

—— (1988). Intellectual development: psychometric and information-processing approaches. In M.H. Bornstein and M.E. Lamb (eds) *Development Psychology: An Advanced Textbook.* Hillsdale, NJ, Erlbaum.

Sternberg, R.J. and Gardner, M.K. (1983). Unities in inductive reasoning. *Journal of Experimental Psychology: General*, 112: 80–116.

Sternberg, R.J. and Rifkin, B. (1979). The development of analogical reasoning processes. *Journal of Experimental Child Psychology*, 27: 195–232.

Stough, C. and Nettlebeck, T. (1989). Letter-inspection time and IQ. *The Psychologist: Bulletin of the British Psychological Society*, 2: 374.

Thorndike, E.L. (1903). *Educational Psychology.* New York, Columbia University Press.

Verster, J.M. (1987). Human cognition and intelligence: towards an integrated theoretical perspective. in S.H. Irvine and S.E. Newstead (ed.) *Intelligence and Cognition: Contemporary Frames of Reference.* Dordrecht, Martinus Nijhoff.

Weinberg, H. (1969). Correlation of frequency spectra of averaged visual evoked potentials with verbal intelligence. *Nature*, 224: 813–15.

Wissler, C. (1901). The correlation of mental and physical tests. *Psychological Review Monograph Supplement*, 3, No. 6.

4

Intelligence in context

At least in the twentieth century, intelligence has been considered to be most manifested in (if not actually to *be*) reasoning or thinking of some sort. Binet, for example, described intelligence as judgement. Spearman (1923) described intelligence as the eduction of relations and correlates. As quasi-mechanical processes, a clear distinction has been drawn between these and the 'knowledge store' on which the reasoning processes are said to act or to call up when necessary (e.g. Kail and Pellegrino 1985). As mentioned in Chapter 2, this is broadly the distinction between 'fluid' and 'crytallised' intelligence, defined by Cattell (1971) and Horn (1982). Smith *et al.* (1988) make the distinction in terms of 'the "mechanics of intelligence"', the relatively content-free architecture of information processing and problem solving'; and 'the application of the mechanics of intelligence to domains of knowledge' (1988: 308).

The IQ and much of the information-processing approach has tended to reduce intelligence to individual differences in the 'strength' or 'power' of reasoning (as we saw in Chapter 3). The presupposition has been that intelligence is simply the variability in the efficiency with which such processes are executed. Thus it has been considered perfectly possible to assess intelligence in an individual, in the form of these quasi-mechanical processes, quite independently of the knowledge which the same person has. The psychometric, and the more recent information-processing and cognitive, searches for intelligence are predicated on such a distinction.

There are many psychologists who have always disputed this distinction even as a remote possibility. In the last decade or so they have been increasingly vindicated. In this chapter we shall be examining these views.

Reasoning in context

Doubts that there exist operations or 'rules' of thought and logic that exist independently of knowledge have been increasing in recent years. One of the most influential critiques has been in the domain of deductive reasoning by Johnson-Laird (1983; 1985). As Johnson-Laird points out, a deduction is a systematic process of thought that leads from a set of propositions to a conclusion implicit in the propositions, for example:

> Joan is taller than Ann
> Ann is taller than Jean
> Therefore Joan is taller than Jean

By virtue of their apparent demand for 'reasoning ability' such problems have long been included in standardised IQ tests, although, as Johnson-Laird (1985: 175) points out, 'Remarkably, psychologists never know what these tests are actually measuring'.

Johnson-Laird's study of deductive reasoning has involved tasks like the Wason Selection Task. In this task subjects are presented with four cards each with some different information on it. They are then dictated a rule which applies to the cards. What they have to do is state which of the four cards it is necessary to turn over to decide whether the rule is being obeyed. For example they may be presented with cards with the following letters or numbers printed on them:

E   K   4   7

The rule might be something like 'If a card has a vowel on one side, then it has an even number on the other side' (Wason and Johnson-Laird 1972; Johnson-Laird 1985). Most subjects get this task wrong, in that they tend to turn over the E (correct) and the 4 (wrong). Only 12 per cent of subjects appreciate the importance of turning over the seven (the only other card that can falsify the rule).

Another version of the task involves more concrete information, and something approximating the real-life context:

Manchester   Sheffield   Train   Car

Rule: 'Every time I go to Manchester I travel by train'. In this task over 60 per cent of subjects appreciated the need to turn over the card with 'Car' on it (if this card had 'Manchester' on it this would negate the rule) (Johnson-Laird 1983).

In a similar task, subjects had to pretend they were postal workers sorting letters, and, given cards analogous to those above, had to determine whether rules like the following were violated: 'If a letter is sealed, then it has a five-penny stamp on it'. In this case 81 per cent of subjects produced the correct responses (Johnson-Laird *et al.* 1972).

Such results, comparing 'realistic' with 'abstract' materials, have been confirmed in a variety of other studies. Thus many subjects err in the following problem (Bruner 1984):

All A's are B's
Are all B's A's?

But few fail when it is put into a meaningful context, like:

All men are mammals
Are all mammals men?

Thus we have the conclusion that reasoning is not something that takes place independently of content or context.

Intelligence in schemes or schemas

Cheng and Holyoak (1985) have argued that reasoning involves abstract knowledge structures induced from life experiences. These represent context-sensitive 'rules' involving predictions from certain preconditions. These structures they call *pragmatic reasoning schemes*. Examples from ordinary social experience include 'permissions', 'obligations' and 'causations'. The schemes involve reasoning; but it is not reasoning independent of a knowledge structure, in the form of a detached 'intelligence': rather the structure of the knowledge and the form of the reasoning are inseparable aspects of the same intelligence.

In this view reasoning, in whatever situation, depends on being able to evoke or 'call up' an appropriate schema, rather than to apply independent powers of intelligence. An arbitrary rule, such as that in the Wason task described above, which is not related to real-life experiences, will not reliably evoke a reasoning schema, and failure will result. On the other hand, when the problem contains a rationale that corresponds with a schema, the schema is invoked and solution follows.

The importance of this 'calling up' of available representations, to mental performance, has been demonstrated in several studies. In experiments in which the Wason task was given either with or without a rationale (e.g. a country's postal regulations governing stamp requirements) it was found that subjects given the rationale performed much better than those who did not (Cheng and Holyoak 1985). Cheng *et al.* (1986) have shown that training in abstract logic does not improve performance on the standard Wason task, whereas even brief 'schema' training, which related the task to some rationale like 'obligation', improved performance markedly. Light *et al.* (1988) found correct performance reaching nearly 80 per cent among 7- to 8-year-olds given a modified version of the Wason task which corresponded to a pragmatic reasoning scheme. Donaldson (1978) has described a number of studies in which children's performance on reasoning tasks became transformed when using familiar materials which made 'human sense'.

Chi and Ceci (1987) criticise the view that performance, even on simple IQ-type tasks like digit span, is independent of background knowledge, and is due instead to processing efficiency, ability or capacity differences. They argue that 'expertise is less a matter of general aptitude than of domain specific knowledge' (1987: 106). What is it that makes expert chess players so superb, for example? In comparing chess experts and novices the predominant factor appears to be sheer quantity of knowledge regarding patterns of pieces and the number of pieces represented in each pattern (Chase and Simon 1973). In some highly practised domains (e.g. computers) particular children may show complex knowledge representation and reasoning that makes them far more 'intelligent' than most adults. As Chi and Glaser (1986) put it, with respect to these and other problem-solving studies, 'It is the problem-solver's representation that guides retrieval of appropriate solution procedures' (1986: 241).

Ceci and Liker (1986) further explored the relation between knowledge and intelligence by examining thirty men who were avid race-goers. Fourteen of these were classified as experts on the basis of their ability to predict starting odds from certain information about horses entered for a race. All the subjects were then asked to handicap horses in ten actual and fifty contrived races. As Ceci and Liker (1986) put it:

> The analyses revealed that expert handicapping was a cognitively sophisticated enterprise, with experts using a mental model that contained multiple interaction effects and nonlinearity. For example, to predict the speed with which a horse could run the final quarter mile of the race, it appears that experts relied on a complex interactive model involving as many as seven variables.
>
> (Ceci and Liker 1986: 255)

Performance in this congitively complex task was unrelated to measured IQ, which leads the authors to conclude that, 'whatever it is that an IQ test measures, it is not the ability to engage in cognitively complex forms of multivariate reasoning' (Ceci and Liker 1986: 265).

Another way in which the role of knowledge in reasoning is displayed is in 'informal', compared with scientific, models of the physical and social world. As mentioned in Chapters 1 and 2, children and untrained adults have 'informal theories' or 'naive concepts' about the world, particularly in the area of 'intuitive physics' (McCloskey 1983; Driver *et al.* 1985) but also in other domains (Carey 1985; Trowbridge and Mintzes 1988). Such informal theories are revealed when subjects are asked to make predictions about relatively simple physical events. For example, subjects are presented with a picture of a man walking and holding a ball at shoulder height. The subjects are asked to indicate the path of the ball when the man lets go of it, and the point where it hits the ground. The correct answer is that it will fall in an arc, but most subjects suggest it will fall downwards in a straight line (McCloskey *et al.* 1983).

Similarly when predicting the trajectory of a bomb falling from an aircraft towards a target subjects tend to do so in such a way that the bomb will miss the target. Subjects believe that a coin or other object tossed upwards has two forces acting on it: the 'force' imparted to it as it is thrown, and which slowly dissipates; and gravity, which acts throughout its movement and eventually 'takes over'. This belief seems to be due to attributing to objects a variable 'force', namely impetus, which they don't actually have and doesn't actually exist (McCloskey and Kargon 1988). Somewhat similar attribution errors have been exposed in people's naive models of social realities, where the behaviour of people is explained in terms of some intuitive model of human nature (Ross 1977; Holland *et al* 1986).

One of the most surprising findings is that successful students of, say, physics or social psychology, who have been taught more circumspect scientific views, often retain these common misconceptions of the world (Clement 1982; Champagne *et al*. 1980). That is, although they have acquired a new, declarative form of knowledge, which, as it were, makes them appear 'intelligent' in the classroom and college, their real-life procedural intelligence continues to be quite different. The difficulties this creates for education have only recently been realised (Driver *et al*. 1985).

Clearly people hang on to these naive conceptions because they appear to be served quite well by them most of the time in the 'here and now'; it is only when we need to go where different conditions prevail that science has to take a hand. But the important point is that here again close inspection has revealed that reasoning is not the independent machination of detached processes, but part of our mental representations of reality. Thus an apparent deficiency in intelligence, as revealed by standardised tests, does not necessarily mean the absence of reasoning processes; it could simply mean the absence of a 'schema' (the intelligence of an individual) which a given unfamiliar task demands. Nor does it mean a deficiency in the ability to *construct* such schemas. This is a point we shall be taking up later in this chapter. First, we need to consider some recent research on knowledge representation which has shown how extraordinarily difficult it is to describe a person's intelligence-qua-knowledge.

Implicit versus explicit knowledge

Recent research into the structure of conceptual representation and reasoning have confirmed a complex duality in knowledge representation that can make us all seem intelligent in certain situations, yet extraordinarily stupid in others. Theorists have had to make a clear distinction between 'implicit' and 'explicit' knowledge.

Much of the knowledge we acquire socially (in school, from books, from other people, for example) consists of simple or complex propositions: the next train from platform 4 is the two-thirty for Waterloo; Na is the symbol for sodium; sodium is a reactive metal; and so on. This is the explicit knowledge that we can encode in the form of everyday language and 'package' for purposes of social transaction and communication. It is sometimes called 'declarative' knowledge, and forms most of the content of the school curriculum.

We can, of course, accumulate considerable quantities of such knowledge in 'rote' fashion. Many (e.g. Edwards and Mercer 1987) argue that most of what pupils learn in school consists of 'ritual' knowledge of this kind. In order to be meaningful such propositions have to reflect a deeper, 'principled' knowledge which is much more complex. This knowledge is abstract in the sense that it involves covariations among numerous variables in ways that are too complex to put into words (Richardson 1990).

Some of the persuasive evidence for the abstract nature of this 'implicit knowledge' comes from experiments in which subjects have to learn artificial grammars – a set of 'rules', such as those in Figure 4.1, capable of producing a set of letter strings. Subjects exposed to exemplars of such strings seem to acquire the grammar underlying it, because they can subsquently distinguish between legitimate and illegitimate strings; but they can rarely put into words what it is they have learned (see Reber 1989 for review; and also Mathews *et al.* 1989).

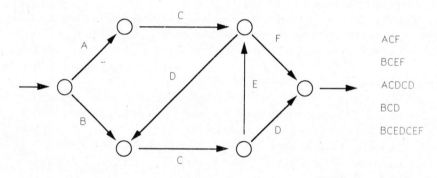

Figure 4.1 Illustration of a Finite State Grammar for studying implicit knowledge and examples of strings it generates by following the arrows through different nodes
Note: See Reber (1989) for more complex grammars and discussion

In somewhat related studies by Broadbent and colleagues (e.g. Berry and Broadbent 1984) subjects had to manipulate a variable in a multivariate situation (e.g. the factors influencing production in a sugar factory modelled on a computer) in order to maximise a given 'output' variable. After trials, subjects had to fill in a questionnaire in which they had to predict the state of an output variable given certain input values. Practice led to significant improvements in management of the task on the computer. But there was no improvement in ability to answer the questionnaires. In other words subjects were quite good at learning the 'deeper' relationships between variables at a practical level; but translating these relations into words was a different matter (see also Berry and Broadbent 1988).

The implications of such studies for intelligence is simply that, as Michael Polanyi (1958) once put it, 'we know more than we can tell'. In situations in which different individuals' implicit knowledge corresponds with the explicit knowledge governing a current social situation, the former maps predictably on to propositions in language or other symbolic forms (explicit knowledge) and expectations are clear to all. In other situations such correspondence may simply not be there. In many testing situations psychologists use tasks and verbal instructions which seem eminently clear to *them*. But these explicit propositions may have no clear counterparts in the implicit knowledge of the subject, whose true intelligence, in consequence, remains untapped *in that situation*.

Note that the view emerging, here, is the opposite to that of Sternberg (1985), who argues that it is precisely 'non-entrenched' tasks that are the best tests of intelligence. Such a view, of course, reflects his belief in intelligence operations or components disconnected from the knowledge store.

> Intelligence is not so much a person's ability to learn or think within conceptual systems that the person has already become familiar with as it is his or her ability to learn and think within new conceptual systems, which can then be brought to bear upon already existing knowledge structure.
>
> (Sternberg 1981: 4, quoted in Sternberg 1984a: 276)

Sternberg's evidence for this consists of performance on certain unusual learning tasks, the results of which correlate moderately with performance on IQ items. His interpretation is that the same latent ability is being tapped in both tests, although there are many other possible explanations of such a correlation. This mechanistic assumption reflects a separation of intelligence (or reasoning) processes from knowledge, in a way that current research is now questioning. What is or is not novel may be relatively easy to identify in explicit knowledge (e.g. the words in familiar, compared with unfamiliar, languages); but in *implicit* knowledge almost every experience may be novel (whatever language we speak, for instance, almost every expression we utter is unique). That is precisely why the knowledge is implicit.

Collins (1989) makes the same point when he notes the difficulty which people experience in following even simple instructions without the prerequisite tacit knowledge. This we can achieve only 'by serving something close to an apprenticeship with an existing expert' (1989: 207). There is a deep paradox, in fact, in not being able to tap a person's implicit intelligence very easily by explicit means. Berry and Broadbent (1989) note that the very nature of implicit knowledge makes it difficult to investigate. They then quote Reber and Lewis (1977) on the acquisition of the implicit knowledge in artificial grammars:

> an annoying kind of uncertainty principle pertains. If we ask our subjects to try to report their cognitive modus operandi during acquisition, the very introspective act transmutes the cognitive process and we lose the implicit element, the very thing we wish to study.
>
> (Reber and Lewis 1977: 334)

Intelligence so difficult to describe, will obviously be extremely difficult to measure, even in well-defined domains such as school history or geography. But human intelligence is not confined to such domains. As humans we all have to learn, from a very early age, the highly abstract rules of living and co-operating with other people in the particular social situations in which we grow up. The vast majority of people acquire and exercise this intelligence with ease.

Intelligence in social context

Although, as humans, virtually everything we do involves other people, both scientists and non-scientists have had a curious tendency to view the behaviour of the individual as the emanation of some internal trait rather than as a product of the social context in which almost any human behaviour is part and parcel. The popular, psychometric notion of intelligence is, *par excellence*, an illustration of this tendency. But it is also a tendency which appears in many information-processing accounts.

The results of this tendency can be seriously misleading. Thus people used to specific social contexts (and whose reasoning reflects that context) always *appear* to be deficient in some internal cognitive power when tested in an unfamiliar context. Gellatly (1989) likens this process of 'cognitive diagnostics' to a 'medical diagnostics' that is seriously awry. As illustration he mentions Seigler's (1976) studies in which a child's successes and failures with a balance-beam problem is characterised in terms of cognitive rules which the child does or does not exhibit. In such problems the child has to predict which side of the balance will swing down, given certain weights in certain positions along the beam. The difficulties which children have with these problems seems to stem from focusing on only one of the two dimensions governing the balancing, namely the weight applied and its distance from the fulcrum. Seigler (1986; c.f. Gellatly 1989) points out that in their everyday social lives (e.g. in their use of language) young children regularly take account of two or more dimensions simultaneously. He argues that they use a single-dimension rule only as a kind of 'fall-back' rule in unfamiliar circumstances.

But, as Gellatly goes on to point out, this is not the 'cause' of their behaviour:

> this rule is Seigler's rule; it is not a rule operated by young children. . . .
> The rule is not inside the individual children, it is part of our way of talking about what they do. The causes of this type of behaviour remain to be formulated, perhaps in terms of unfamiliar problems inducing heightened arousal that results in attentional rigidity.
>
> (Gellatly 1989: 125)

Imputing to children the lack of a general 'power' on the basis of a highly localised test is a common tendency of psychologists. For example, Sternberg

(1988: 286), on the basis of highly specific test scores, argues that 'Almost all children will eventually walk . . . but not all children becomes, say, adept analogical reasoners or spatial visualisers'. Yet analogical reasoning and spatial visualising (however we characterise them) are surely such an intrinsic part of even the very young child's social-behavioural organisation, that it is difficult to see how the simplest performances like play, and object and event recognition, or drawing inferences from the partial pictorial information in books or magazines, would be possible without them. And when we remind ourselves that the test scores seem to be related to nothing of importance beyond the simple fact of predicting school performance, it seems likely that we are being dangerously selectively in our attention to information about children's abilities.

Ross (1977) has called such beliefs – that the causes of behaviours lie in the dispositions of the individual rather than in the nature of the situation confronting the individual – the 'fundamental attribution error'. Much research confirms casual observation that individuals tend to explain *other people's* behaviour in terms of individual traits. It is surely instructive that people tend to explain their *own* behaviour in terms of social constraints and expectations (Holland *et al.* 1986).

In sum, reasoning appears to be embedded not only in mental representations of physical contexts, but even more so in representations of *social* contexts. This point has been made by a number of theorists since the 1930s and has been the subject of more recent empirical studies.

In the western world, the point that human thought and action go on in a social framework was put most strongly by George Herbert Mead (1934). As Blumer (1965–6) explains about Mead's view:

> Everywhere we look in human society we see people engaging in forms of joint-action. Indeed, the totality of such instances – in all of their multitudinous variety, their variable connections, and their complex networks – constitutes the life of a society. It is easy to understand from these remarks why Mead saw joint action, or the social act, as the distinguishing characteristic of society.
>
> (Blumer 1965–6: 538)

It is not too far-fetched to argue that the intellectual demands of such complex social activity far outstrips that required in the average IQ test item, yet the vast majority of children become competent in such activities from a very early age.

A theorist who has become well known in this respect is L.S. Vygotsky, a Soviet psychologist who died at an early age in the 1930s, but whose writings have more recently become available in the west (see e.g. Vygotsky 1962; 1978; Wertsch 1985). Vygotsky argued that all our cognitive functions are largely determined by the way we co-operate, as humans, with others in all our activities. Such co-operation is mediated through various 'tools'. These include practical tools such as hammers, machines, and so on; communicational tools such as spoken and written language; computational tools and procedures for problem-solving; and a host of 'institutional' rules that regulate our social interactions, including industrial and agricultural production, the law, the family, and other social institutions.

Since it is through these that we invariably act, they dominate the way we think, i.e. our intelligence.

> By being included in the process of behaviour, the psychological tool alters the entire flow and structure of mental functions. It does this by determining the structure of a new instrumental act just as a technical tool alters the process of natural adaptation by determining the form of labour operation.
>
> (Vygotsky 1981: 137)

In this view there is 'intelligence' as an identifiable human character, that is as an organising principle of human social thought and activity; but there is no such 'thing' as intelligence as an individual character separate from social context: 'the very mechanism underlying higher mental functions is a copy from social interaction; all higher mental functions are internalised social relationships' (Vygotsky 1981: 161).

According to this theory, the primary source of the 'rules' of reasoning lie in the pattern of social interactions through which we produce and otherwise behave in the world; only secondarily do they come to reside in the heads of individuals, that is, they arise 'interpsychologically' before manifesting themselves 'intrapsychologically' (Newman *et al.* 1989). To find evidence of this Newman *et al.* (1989) looked for a schema they might study in a peer-interactional setting. Schoolchildren, in groups of two or three, were presented with four chemicals in bottles and asked to mix all possible pairs of combinations in the test tubes provided and observe and note the results. (The chemicals are chosen so as to exhibit interesting results, like changing colour, when mixed.)

The conventional 'schema' for this kind of task is what Newman *et al.* call an 'intersection schema', namely a systematic combination of the form 1+2, 1+3, 1+4, 2+3, etc. This schema was never used by the children in this way, but it was present none the less. The children had no problems devising all possible combinations, and the intersection schema was employed as a *checking* procedure in various ways by different groups. For example, one member of the group would check for all the 1s, another for all the 2s, and so on. As Newman *et al.* (1989) note:

> The intersection schema thus regulated the interaction among the children as part of the context that regulates the individual actions . . . the intersection schema is not just, or even primarily, an *internal knowledge* structure. It is also importantly locatable *in the interaction among the children*. It is, in Vygotsky's terminology, an *interpsychological* cognitive process.
>
> (Newman *et al.* 1989: 48–9, italics in original)

In reality, of course (as these investigators point out), there is a dialectical relation between the individual's representation(s) and the social representation which is the seat of knowledge and action. We shall discuss the development of this 'intelligence' further in Chapter 5.

Many of the sentiments in Vygotsky's theorising have been incorporated into a new discipline called 'social cognition' (see e.g. Butterworth and Light 1982). The upshot of these studies is that people's reasoning goes on in the context of 'social schemas'. People's true cognitive abilities are revealed only in situations which make sense to them as meaningful problems in a social context which recruit those schemas.

Most investigations in this new framework have been done with children. An example is a series of experiments using Piaget's conservation task (e.g. Piaget 1952; see also Chapter 5 for further discussion of Piaget). In this task a child may, for example, be confronted with two identical beakers, which are partially filled with liquid to the same levels. The child is asked to agree about the equality of the amounts of liquid. Next, the contents of one of the beakers is poured into another of a different shape. The child is again asked about the equality of the amounts of liquid (see Figure 4.2).

The typical result from such a procedure is that children below 7–8 years will agree that the initial amounts of liquid are the same, but no longer remain the same after one has been poured into the other glass. (Older children agree about the equality of amounts throughout.) The conclusion drawn from Piaget and others is that younger children are incapable of reasoning properly, in failing to 'conserve' the amounts; in Piagetian terms they don't have 'operational intelligence' yet (see Chapter 5 for more on this).

McGarrigle and Donaldson (1975), suspecting social-contextual factors at play in this procedure, tried a slight modification of the task. They first tried the standard procedure, as described above. Then they tried a modified condition in which a 'naughty teddy', manipulated by the experimenter, rushed about and, in the process, accidentally rearranged the materials. The children were then asked about the equality of the materials as before. Only 16 per cent of children gave 'conserving answers' in the standard condition. Although the physical stimuli and the questions asked of the children were exactly the same in the second condition, this time 63 per cent of subjects gave conserving answers. Similar results have been found in other studies using different procedures (see Light 1986 for review).

The upshot of these studies is that children fail to reason as expected in the standard conservation task, not because they lack reasoning powers, but because the task fails to make 'human sense' to them. The intentions of the experimenter to them are particularly confusing. When a rationale (such as an 'accident') underlying the transformation of the materials is clear to them, childen's reasoning, even among 5-year-olds, improves dramatically.

A number of more recent studies have indicated the subtle ways in which the ease or difficulty of a mental task can be affected by whether or not it maps on to social rules or schemas familiar to the individual (Light and Perret-

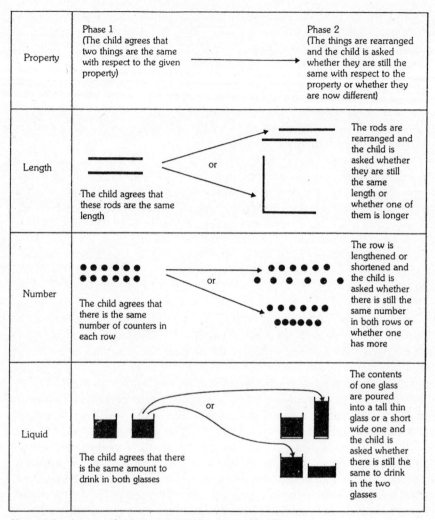

Figure 4.2   Some typical 'conservation' tasks used by Piaget
Source: Reproduced with permission of the Open University

Clermont 1989). Such observations are beginning to revise seriously our notions of cognitive competence. As Light (1986) points out:

> We see here the beginnings of a shift in which the social context moves from having the status of a performance variable, simply limiting the expression of the child's competence, towards a more central and constitutive role.

> (Light 1986: 234)

In this socio-historical view, therefore, individuals are intelligent to the extent that they have acquired knowledge of the world as it is embedded in the tacit rules of social activities in which they participate.

> The usual function of the hammer, for example, is not understood by exploring the hammer itself (although the child may discover some facts about weight and balance). The child's appropriation of culturally devised 'tools' comes about through involvement in culturally organized activities in which the tool plays a role.
>
> (Newman *et al*, 1989: 63)

Let us apply this social-psychological perspective to the lone child struggling single-handed with a Raven's Matrices item. To the psychologist it is just a 'task' to which must be applied whatever 'mechanics' of intelligence the child is endowed with. The kind of analyses presented above, however, would suggest that, to the unfortunate subject, it is many other things as well. First and foremost, it is a social situation which has to make 'human sense' to the child. In grappling with thoughts like 'What is expected of me here?', and with possible panic over the knowledge that it is a *test*, certain stimuli – the language of the tester; the pencil and paper; the very form of presentation; in other words, what Karmiloff-Smith (1984) calls a 'representational handle' – may trigger appropriate schemes or schemas in some children, but not in others.

The point is that describing people's mental abilities requires far more sensitivity to the social context in which abilities develop and are expressed. This is because the situation is rarely simply a 'task'. It almost invariably involves other people, and therefore reasoning about their expectations and intentions, which in turn demands experiential knowledge of similar social interactions. As Wells (1986) put it,

> under normal circumstances of interaction, the focus of our attention is not on the verbal and nonverbal messages through which we communicate our intentions, but rather on the intentions themselves in relation to the specific activity in which we and our co-participants are engaged.
>
> (Wells 1986: 141)

The ability to respond to any specific task, therefore, consists of complex socio-cognitive-experiential representations that are difficult to grade in any operational or mechanical sense. Heath (1986), for example, describes how many children are socialised, through the use of books in the family, to 'decontextualise' themselves from the topic in information exchange at a very early age. This was illustrated by one middle-class child who, before the age of 2, had 'learned to manipulate the context of items, her own activities, and language to achieve booklike, decontextualised, repeatable effects (such as puns)' (Heath 1986: 104). This schema contrasts with the 'social and cognitive aims in other sociocultural groups' that do not have 'this finely-tuned, constant, repetitive, and continuous pattern of training' (1986: 105).

Keating and MacLean (1987) made this kind of point about claims that tests like the Raven's Matrices assess decontextualised mental mechanisms, and are therefore 'culture-free' or 'culture-fair'. Instead, they argued, such tests can be said to 'tap highly formal and specific school skills related to text processing and decontextualised rule application, and are thus the most *systematically acculturated* tests' (1987: 243, italics in original). In other words, variation across individuals reflects '*the degree of acculturation to the mainstream school skills of Western society*' (1987: 244, italics in original).

Ironically the idea of the test as a complex social situation is certainly not new. According to Brett's *History of Psychology*, Binet himself discusses (1900)

> how the form of a question tends to determine the psychological reaction expressed in the answer; children were found particularly to fabricate answers, not by deliberate falsehood, but by the construction of 'memories' and ideas which were due to the pressure being put upon them by the fact of being questioned.

(Peters 1953: 503)

Thus it seems reasonable to argue that even the most culture-free intelligence tests and test situations cannot be described as 'pure' cognitive tasks isolated from a social context. The constitutive role of social context in intelligence becomes even clearer when we examine the issue of intelligence-as-reasoning in different cultures.

Intelligence and culture

A large number of studies have pointed to the difficulty of assessing intelligence detached from socio-cultural context. Some of these have merely pointed to the unfamiliarity of test materials or of test-taking situations. Sometimes this results in a complete failure to play the game of the investigator. Johnson-Laird (1985) illustrates this with a member of the Kpelle people living in Liberia studied by Scribner (1977). Given the following deductive reasoning problem,

> All Kpelle men are rice farmers
> Mr Smith is not a rice farmer
> Is he a Kpelle man?

the subject just kept replying that he didn't know the man, therefore he couldn't answer the question. As Johnson-Laird (1985) points out, this is not due to any lack of reasoning powers. The subject is actually making a deduction:

> All the deductions that I can make are about individuals that I know
> I do not know Mr Smith
> Therefore I cannot make a deduction about Mr Smith.

The deduction is simply not the one that is being sought by the investigator.

It was observations such as this that led Sternberg (1985) to propose a 'contextual subtheory' of intelligence. 'The contextual subtheory specifies the potential set of contents for behaviours that can be characterised as intelligent.

It addresses the question of which behaviours are intelligent for whom, and where these behaviours are intelligent' (1984a: 269). Thus it recognises that what counts as intelligence will not be the same among Australian Aborigines, say, as among London stockbrokers.

But it is not clear that the hypothesis of culture as *constitutive* of human intelligence is being grasped here. Sternberg's theory appears to propose cultural *criteria* for the identification or evaluation of intelligence (ones that take into account cultural settings) rather than viewing culture as constitutive of intelligence itself. There is still, according to this theory, an intelligence 'within' the individual that is different from the context 'without'. Sternberg's contextual theory, that is,

> deals with the interface between intelligence and the *external* contexts that impinge upon, and are impinged upon by, intelligence. The contextual position needs to be supplemented by a mechanistic theory of the mental structures and processes that constitute intelligent thought.
>
> (Sternberg 1984b: 31)

These contexts appear to be, in Sternberg's terms, factors to be taken into account in getting at the 'real' intelligence underneath its cultural clothing.

The argument, of course, boils down to one concerning the degree of 'cultural relativity' in the make-up of intelligence. Many, like Sternberg, believe in something universal, isolable and measurable through any particular cultural pattern. 'I believe that there are many aspects of intelligence that transcend cultural boundaries, and that are, in fact, universal' (1984a: 274). Others question whether culture can be considered as simply a set of constraints on the expression of 'true' intelligence (Laboratory of Comparative Human Cognition 1982; Scribner 1986), although the search for universal principles of some sort, and cultural relativity, may not be entirely incompatible, as Berry (1984) points out.

The alternative view emphasises that culture is not a set of 'means' conveniently available to the individual whose 'true' intelligence will shine through, no matter what the specific means are. The shared psychological structures or programmes that make up a culture are not just 'media' which a prior intelligence comes to use through accidents of birth and upbringing. These programmes, in dialectical relation with the individual mind, *constitute* the intelligence. As Collins (1989) put it,

> society is the basic knowledge-bearing unit, not the individuals within it. The theory fits well with the routine observations that people living in different sorts of societies develop different kinds of skill – they have different cognitions in different social worlds – and that people who are not members of a society that embodies a certain skill have immense difficulty in learning that skill.
>
> (Collins 1989: 206)

Further support for this general argument comes from archaeological and anthropological studies of human evolution.

Intelligence in evolutionary context

This story goes roughly as follows (see Leakey 1979; Wood 1978; Holloway 1975; Piatelli-Palmarini 1989 for reviews). Humans evolved from tree-dwelling primates at least 15 million years ago when the forests thinned, and occupation of the open savannah was forced upon them. This made them vulnerable to attack from savage carnivores, and the only plentiful food supply was large game. Thus arose intense selection pressures for the evolution of a quite unique degree of social co-operation for defensive and hunting purposes. But co-operation to this extent is very demanding in terms of the extra volume, complexity and fine-grainedness of information that has to be processed by the nervous system. Thus also arose selection pressures for a reconstructed and bigger 'social brain' that could become attuned, somehow, to these social ways.

In fact, following adoption of these social ways, the human brain tripled in size in a very short space of time; a quite remarkable phenomenon in its own right (see E.G. Bilsborough 1976). The important point for human intelligence, however, is that this evolution *followed* the adoption of a social life, that is human intelligence has been the *result* of a social life; the latter is not the deliberate product of superior intelligence.

> It would now appear . . . that the large size of the brain of certain hominids was a relatively late development and that the brain evolved due to new selection pressures after bipedalism and consequent upon the use of tools. The tool-using, ground-living, hunting way of life created the large human brain rather than large brained man discovering certain new ways of life. . [We] believe this conclusion is the most important result of the recent fossil hominid discoveries and is one which carries far-reaching implications for the interpretation of human behaviour and its origins.
>
> (Washburn and Howell 1960: 50)

It is in this sense that culture is constitutive of – not merely a product of – human intelligence. As Geertz (1962) put it,

> man's nervous system does not merely enable him to acquire culture, it positively demands that he do so if it is going to function at all. Rather than culture acting only to supplement, develop and extend organically based capacities . . . it would seem to be ingredient to those capacities themselves. A cultureless human being would probably turn out to be not an intrinsically talented though unfulfilled ape, but a wholly mindless and consequently unworkable monstrosity. Like the cabbage it so much resembles, the Homo sapiens brain, having arisen within the framework of human culture, would not be viable outside of it.
>
> (Geertz 1962: 723–4)

According to this view at its strongest, culture is not so much the context in which individual intelligence flourishes and finds expression. Rather the evolved human brain is the context in which co-operative social relations can develop and function as brilliantly as they have done. Its function is the grasp of symbols and other social conventions and a continuous concern for others' interests, intentions and actions. As Travarthen and Logotheti (1989: 37) point out, 'This kind of intelligence is different from any social intelligence of animals, even that of apes'. Intelligence in this sense does not merely consist of individually efficient cognitive processes. It consists of the shared 'tools' and activities mentioned by Vygotsky and others.

Cultures are ingredient to mental activities and constitutive of intelligence because they are the patterns of activity in which we all participate in order to exist. These patterns include the way we relate together to produce our basic necessities; the precise subdivision of our actions and that of our co-participants in the total pattern; the diversity of institutions (employment, law, education, etc.) regulating these subdivisions; the tools, implements or machines that we use in the process; the distribution of authority, property and power; the 'rules' which sanction such a distribution; the way we relate in marriage patterns, kinship patterns, religious and symbolic practices, and so on. It seems naive to think that the patterns of thought and their variability might be somehow independent of these, or that there is something 'deeper' and universal that can be identified as 'true' intelligence beneath them.

But cultures are very complex organisations as well. Given the way that human groups interact and are interdependent, it is highly unlikely that there are any isolated or 'pure' cultures. By the same token, any modern industrialised society is a complex of overlapping cultures and subcultures, and most members of a given society will belong to several of these at the same time, so that people will be differentiated, culturally, on a graded, rather than an all-or-none basis. This, together with the notion of the dialectical relation between individual and culture, mitigates an extreme cultural relativism. As Newman *et al* (1989) put it, we must 'welcome . . . multiple representations as a natural consequence of the social construction of knowledge' (1989: 136). To call that variation 'intelligence', in the sense of some intrinsic mechanical property of the individual, seems to deny the nature of culture and of the dialectical relation between individual and culture.

References

Berry, J.W. (1984). Towards a universal psychology of cognitive competence. In P. Fry (ed.) *Changing Conceptions of Intelligence and Intellectual Functioning: Current Theory and Research*. Amsterdam, North-Holland.

Berry, D.C. and Broadbent, D.E. (1988). Interactive tasks and the implicit–explicit distinction. *British Journal of Psychology*, 79: 251–72.

—— (1989). On the relationship between task performance and associated verbalized knowledge. *Quarterly Journal of Experimental Psychology*, 36A: 209–31.

Bilsborough, A. (1976). *Beyond the Information Given*. London, George Allen & Unwin.

Blumer, H. (1965–6). Sociological implications of the thought of George Herbert Mead. *American Journal of Sociology*, 71, 535–44.

Bruner, J.S. (1974). Patterns of evolution in Middle Pleistocene hominids. *Journal of Human Evolution*, 5: 423–39.

Butterworth, G.E. and Light, P. (eds) (1982) *Social Cognition: Studies in the Development of Understanding*. Brighton, Harvester.

Carey, S. (1985). Conceptual change in childhood. Cambridge, Mass., MIT Press.

Cattell, R.B. (1971). *Abilities: Their Growth, Structure and Action*. Boston, Houghton-Mifflin.

Ceci, S.J. and Liker, J.K. (1986). A day at the races: a study of IQ, expertise and cognitive complexity. *Journal of Experimental Psychology: General*, 115: 255–66.

Champagne, A.B., Klopfer, L.E. and Anderson, J.H. (1980). Factors influencing the learning of classical mechanics. *American Journal of Physics*, 48: 1,074–9.

Chase, W.G. and Soimon, H.A. (1973). Perception in chess. *Cognitive Psychology*, 4: 55–81.

Cheng, P.W. and Holyoak, K.J. (1985). Pragmatic reasoning schemes. *Cognitive Psychology*, 17: 391–416.

Cheng, P.W., Holyoak, K.J., Nisbett, R.E. and Oliver, L.M. (1986). Pragmatic versus syntactic approaches to training deductive reasoning. *Cognitive Psychology*, 18: 293–328.

Chi, M.T.H. and Ceci, S.J. (1987). Content knowledge: its role in representation and restructuring in memory development. *Advances in Child Development and Behaviour*, 20: 91–142.

Chi, M.T.H. and Glaser, R. (1985). Problem solving ability. In R.J. Sternberg (ed.) *Human Abilities: An Information Processing Approach*. New York, Freeman.

Collins, H.M. (1989). Learning through enculturation. In A. Gellatly, D. Rogers and J.A. Sloboda (eds) *Cognition and Social Worlds*. Oxford, Clarendon.

Donaldson, M. (1978). *Children's Minds*. London, Fontana.

Driver, R., Guesne, E. and Tiberghien, A. (eds) (1985). *Children's Ideas in Science*. Milton Keynes, Open Univesity Press.

Edwards, D. and Mercer, N. (1987). *Common Knowledge*. London, Methuen.

Gellatly, A. (1989). The myth of cognitive diagnostics. In A. Gellatly, D. Rogers and J.A. Sloboda (eds) *Cognition and Social Worlds*. Oxford, Clarendon.

Heath, S. (1986). What no bedtime story means: narrative skills at home and at school. In B.B. Scheiffelin and E. Ochs (eds) *Language Socialisation Across Cultures*. Cambridge, Cambridge University Press.

Holland, J.H., Holyoak, K.J. Nisbett, R.E. and Thagard, P.R. (1986). *Induction: Processes of Inference, Learning and Discovery*. Cambridge, Mass., MIT Press.

Holloway, R.L. (1975). *The Role of Human Social Behavior in the Evolution of the Brain*. New York, American Museum of Natural History.

Horn, J.L. (1982). The theory of fluid and crystallised intelligence in relation to concepts of cognitive psychology and ageing in adulthood. In F.I.M. Craik and S. Trehub (eds) *Ageing and Cognitive Processes*. Boston, Plenum.

Johnson-Laird, P.N. (1983). *Mental Models*. Cambridge, Mass., Harvard University Press.

——— (1985). Deductive reasoning ability. In R.J. Sternberg (ed.) *Human Abilities*. New York, Freeman.

Johnson-Laird, P.N., Legrenzi, P. and Legrenzi, S.M. (1972). Reasoning and a sense of reality. *British Journal of Psychology*, 63: 395–400.

Kail, R. and Pellegrino, J.W. (1985). *Human Intelligence: Perspectives and Prospects*. New York, Freeman.

Karmiloff-Smith, A. (1984). Children's problem solving. In M.E. Lamb, A.L. Brown and B. Rogoff (eds) *Advances in Developmental Psychology*, vol. 3. Hillsdale, NJ, Erlbaum.

Keating, D.P. and MacLean, D.J. (1987). Cognitive processing, cognitive ability and development: a reconsideration. In P.A. Vernon (ed.) *Speed of Information Processing and Intelligence*. New York, Ablex.

Laboratory of Comparative Human Cognition (1982). Culture and intelligence. In R.J. Sternberg (ed.) *Handbook of Human Intelligence*, vol. 2. Cambridge, Cambridge University Press.

Leakey, R. (1979). *People of the Lake: Mankind and its Beginnings*. New York, Doubleday.

Light, P. (1986). Context, conservation and conversation. In M. Richards and P. Light (eds) *Children of Social Worlds*. Cambridge, Polity.

Light, P. and Perret-Clermont, A.-N. (1989). in A. Gellatly, D. Rogers and J.A. Sloboda (eds) *Cognition and Social Worlds*. Oxford, Clarendon.

Light, P., Blaye, A., Gilly, M. and Girotto, V. (1988). *Pragmatic Schemes and Logical Reasoning in Six to Eight Year Olds*. Occasional Papers, 88/1, Centre for Human Development and Learning. The Open University.

McCloskey, M. (1983). Intuitive physics. *Scientific American*, 24: 122–30.

McCloskey, M. and Kargon, R. (1988). The meaning and use of historical models in the study of intuitive physics. In S. Strauss (ed.) *Ontogeny, Phylogeny and Historical Development*. NJ, Ablex.

McGarrigle, J. and Donaldson, M. (1975). Conservation accidents. *Cognition*, 3: 341–50.

Mathews, R.C., Buss, R.R., Stanley, W.B., Blanchard-Fields, F., Cho, J.R. and Druhan, B. (1989). Role of implicit and explicit processes in learning from exemplars: a synergistic effect. *Journal of Experimental Psychology: Learning, Memory and Cognition*, 15: 1,083-100.

Mead, G.H. (1934). *Mind, Self and Society*. Chicago, University of Chicago Press.

Newman, D., Griffin, P. and Cole, M. (1989). *The Construction Zone: Working for Cognitive Change in School*. Cambridge, Cambridge University Press.

Peters, R.S. (ed.) (1953). *Brett's History of Psychology*. Cambridge, Mass., MIT Press.

Piaget, J. (1952). *The Origins of Intelligence in Children*. New York, International Universities Press.

Piatelli-Palmarini, M. (1989). Evolution, selection and cognition. *Cognition*, 31: 1-44.

Polanyi, M. (1958). *Personal Knowledge: Towards a Critical Philosophy*. Chicago, University of Chicago Press.

Reber, A.S. (1989). Implicit learning and tacit knowledge. *Journal of Experimental Psychology: General*, 118: 219–35.

Reber, A.S. and Lewis, S. (1977). Toward a theory of implicit learning: the analysis of the form and structure of a body of tacit knowledge. *Cognition*, 5: 333-61.

Reynolds, V. (1976). *The Biology of Human Action*. Reading, Mass., Freeman.

Richardson, K. (1990). The abstraction of covariation in conceptual representation. *British Journal of Psychology* (in press).

Ross, J. (1977). The intuitive psychologist and his shortcomings. In L. Berkowitz (ed.) *Advances in Experimental Social Psychology*, vol. 10. New York, Academic Press.

Scribner, S. (1977). Modes of thinking and ways of speaking: culture and logic reconsidered. In P.N. Johnson-Laird and P.C. Wason (eds) *Thinking: Readings in Cognitive Science*. Cambridge, Cambridge University Press.

—— (1986). Thinking in action: some characteristics of practical thought. In R.J. Sternberg and R.K. Wagner (eds) *Practical Intelligence*. Cambridge, Cambridge University Press.

Seigler, R.S. (1976). Three aspects of cognitive development. *Cognitive Psychology*, 8: 481–520.

—— (1983). Information processing approaches to cognitive development. In W. Kessen (ed.) *Handbook of Child Psychology*, vol. 1. New York, Wiley.

—— (1986). *Children's Thinking*. Englewood Cliffs, NJ, Prentice-Hall.

Smith, J., Dixon, R.A. and Baltes, P.B. (1988). Expertise in life-planning: a new research approach to investigating aspects of wisdom. In M.L. Commons, J.D. Swift, F.A. Richards and C. Armou (eds) *Advances in Development, VI: Comparisons and Applications of Developmental Models*. New York, Praeger.

Spearman, C. (1923). *The Nature of 'Intelligence' and the Principles of Cognition*. London, Macmillan.

Sternberg, R.J. (1981). Intelligence and nonentrenchment. *Journal of Educational Psychology*, 73: 1–16.

—— (1984a). Toward a triarchic theory of human intelligence. *Behavioral and Brain Sciences*, 7: 269-315.

—— (1984b). A contextualist view of the nature of intelligence. In P.S. Fry (ed.) *Changing Conceptions of Intelligence and Intellectual Functioning: Current Theory and Research*. Amsterdam, North-Holland.

—— (1985). *Beyond IQ: A Triarchic Theory of Human Intelligence*. Cambridge, Cambridge University Press.

Trevarthen, C. and Logotheti, K. (1989). Child and culture: genesis of cooperative knowing. In A. Gellatly, D. Rogers and J.A. Sloboda (eds) *Cognition and Social Worlds*. Oxford, Clarendon.

Trowbridge, J.E. and Mintzes, J.J. (1988). Alternative conceptions in animal classification: a cross-age study. *Journal of Research in Science Teaching*, 25: 547–71.

Vygotsky, L.S. (1962). *Thought and Language*, Cambridge, Mass., MIT Press.

—— (1978). *Mind in Society*. (Edited by M. Cole, V. John-Steiner,. S. Scribner and E. Souberman.) Cambridge, Mass., Harvard University Press.

—— (1981). The instrumental method in psychology. In J.V. Wertsch (ed.) *The Concept of Activity in Soviet Psychology*. New York, M.E. Sharpe.

Washburn, S.L. and Howell, F.C. (1960). Human evolution and culture. In S. Tax (ed.) *The Evolution of Man*. Chicago, Ill., University of Chicago Press.

Wason, P.C. and Johnson-Laird, P.N. (1972). *Psychology of Reasoning: Structure and Content*. London, Batsford.

Wells, G. (1986). The language experience of five year old children at home and at school. In J. Cook-Gumperz (ed.) *The Social Construction of Literacy*. Cambridge, Cambridge University Press.

Wertsch, J.V. (ed.) (1985). *Culture, Communication and Cognition: Vygotskyan Perspectives.* Cambridge, Cambridge University Press.

Wood, B.A. (1978). *Human Evolution.* London, Chapman and Hall.

5

Intelligence in development

Development is an unexpectedly complicated topic in any domain. A popular view, and some dictionary definitions, see development merely as a process of growth: simply getting bigger. Some psychologists, by presupposing that intelligence is a more or less fixed 'quantifiable' entity present at birth, view the development of intelligence in this way; that what is 'intelligence' merely increases with age and individual differences at birth persist, except that the 'gap' between individuals may increase. Thus development is a process of *maturation*. Since the psychometric view of intelligence presupposes just such a fixed entity present at birth, with predetermined variation of values among individuals, psychometric descriptions of development consist of showing how children ranked early in life maintain their ranks in later life.

In another view this is not development at all. The developmental geneticist C.H. Waddington (1970) drew attention to the complex issues involved in describing development. Development proper (as opposed to mere growth), he maintained, is a 'progressive sequence of changes' (1970: 185). By this he meant the complex differentiation and reorganisation of structures and processes, which can be such that the final outcome may hardly resemble the initial state at all. If intelligence is something that *develops*, rather than just matures, therefore, we are faced with an enormous paradox. How do we describe in purely observational terms (let alone theoretical terms) something that is always changing?

The problem is even greater if we wish to obtain a measure of intelligence at different stages of development. By definition, what we are measuring at different stages is not the same thing. And if different children develop differently at all, then it is difficult to *compare* them on the same scale. Psychometric testers have got over this problem in the past by selecting items and constructing tests such that average performances increase gradually with age. This in turn has created an illusion of 'growth' of intelligence that matches their own maturationist presuppositions.

A number of developmental psychologists, however, have pointed to the dangers inherent in such an approach. If development (as opposed to mere maturation) occurs, it follows that we ought to be measuring something different at different ages and stages. But we cannot know what that 'something different' is without a clear description of development in advance.

> The determination of age differences assumes that the measuring instrument yield scores that are comparable in the sense of measuring qualitatively equivalent capacities or behaviour. If, for example, we use one battery of sub-tests for measuring intelligence at age four, and different batteries at age six, eight, ten, twelve and fourteen, plotting scores against chronological age assumes that all of the batteries are equally representative of general intelligence.
>
> (Ausubel and Sullivan 1970: 25)

In fact, even within the existing psychometric data, there is considerable evidence that things don't remain the same (Verster 1987). In reviewing some of this evidence, Sternberg (1988) suggests the following possibilities:

1 Breakdown of a unitary factor into more specific or group factors with age. Evidence for this, he suggests, is that intercorrelations between different subtests of IQ tests decrease with age.
2 Evidence from factor analyses of growth study data that different factors are more important (i.e. contribute to more of the variance) at different ages. This implies the view that what we call intelligence, in IQ, is not the same thing at different developmental ages.

Even allowing for the vagaries of factor analysis (see Chapter 2) both of these would be expected if intelligence indeed develops rather than simply matures.

Our presuppositions about development will inevitably be conditioned by our view of intelligence in general. But what we presuppose will also have implications for our scientific aspirations – the level of descriptive and theoretical complexity we are willing to accept as a good account of development. Thus if we presuppose that intelligence (*qua* individual differences) merely matures, we are likely to settle for the plotting of plausible test scores against age, and possibly correlations among these. Such plots or correlations will show the consistency/deviation of scores across age groups. Then we can speculate whether this stability/instability is the result of environmental perturbations; of different genetic expressions at different ages; or whatever. In the past many psychologists have seen this as a useful thing to do (see Figure 5.1), and this is still the case today. Thus Seitz (1988) argues that the 'two chief aims in development research are determining what is typical behaviour at different ages . . . and studying the stability of behaviour across time'. As already argued, this is really the study of non-development.

If we presuppose, on the other hand, that intelligence genuinely *develops* we shall require a detailed description of the *changes* in question at the times they occur. If we want a *theory* of development, then we need an account of the developing *system* (mentioned in Chapter 1) which includes not only the components and properties involved in the whole system, but also the inter-relations between them: what changes, when, into what, and what other factors are involved in the direction and magnitude of change, and how? When we have this kind of theory we can make predictions about development, given certain circumstances; explain a given state of development in terms of past circumstances; or intervene in circumstances in order to promote development.

All of these questions are reflected, to some extent, in the accounts which follow. Before introducing them, the point has to be made that we do not yet have finely honed developmental theories of the ideal kind just mentioned. Rather they are mixtures of assumption, presupposition and intriguing obser-vation which are still mainly in the inductive stage of theory construction. Little testing of a rigorous hypothetico-deductive kind has been done on any of them. Obviously since there is little agreement about the nature of the subject itself, there can be little agreement about a *description*, let alone a theory, of its development. In consequence, the appeal, to the reader, of the accounts below, is more likely to consist of a combination of plausibility and prejudice, than of scientific detachment.

General form of growth or development of IQ

The way in which Binet-type IQ tests are constructed ensures that they con-tain their own 'development' (i.e. growth) pattern – a specific growth pattern is built-in, and any age differences are not an objective description of the de-velopment of intelligence. To understand this, let us go back to Binet's meth-od. By trying out the original items on 200 children between the ages of 3 and 15 it was found that the percentage of each age group passing was not the same from item to item. That is some were apparently more difficult than others (which is what Binet had intended in selecting the items).

Binet considered the good items to be those on which the percentage passing increased rapidly from year to year. Accordingly the different items were age-graded by considering the percentage of each age group passing each particular item. Thus if a particular item was passed by, say, 75 per cent of 8-year-olds it was considered to be a test of 8-year-old intelligence. By such means the tests were grouped according to age: if a child passed the tests from those intended for 3-year-olds through to those grouped as 9-year-old tests, then he or she was considered to have a mental age of 9 years. The same principles guided the revisions of the Binet test (in the form of the Stanford-Binet) and virtually all other IQ tests since.

It is not difficult to see that as children get older they will tend to get higher scores: children automatically follow a course of growth in 'intelligence' in such tests. Indeed the kind of graph shown in Figure 5.1 has frequently been obtained by testing children of different ages, or the same group of children followed and retested at intervals over several years (Bayley 1970). But this is not an independent description of the development of intelligence; it is simply an inevitable consequence of the way the test is constructed. We would, of course, expect intelligence to increase over the span of several years. But few characters, physical or psychological, develop in a smooth curve like this; characters like height, brain size or vocabulary develop unevenly or in 'spurts'.

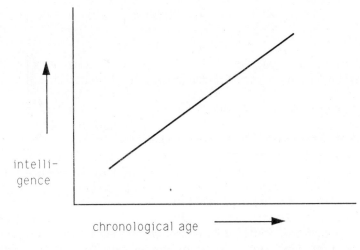
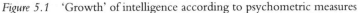

Figure 5.1   'Growth' of intelligence according to psychometric measures

Again, apparently objective empirical data are simply artefacts of prior decisions about the nature of intelligence. Failure to realise this has had many controversial repercussions in the psychometric literature. One of these is the lifelong curve of IQ against age. This shows IQ on standardised tests such as the Raven's Matrices and the Wechsler increasing steadily with age up to about 18 years. But then it apparently starts falling again (see Figure 5.2; see e.g. Butcher 1968; Schaie and Herzog 1986; Smith *et al.* 1988, for further discussion). Some psychologists have taken this to be a 'true' picture of the development of intelligence in youth and adulthood, in spite of the fact that, as many others have argued, the human intelligence of 'real life' continues to increase well beyond that age. As Garcia (1972) pointed out:

> While a person's ability to handle school items declines after he [sic] leaves school, his ability to deal with the rest of the world often improves. . . . If we search for other items that reflect greater capacity for dealing with the postschool environments and blend these items with the school and preschool items, we will discover that intelligence continues to grow beyond the high-school years.
>
> (Garcia 1972: 43)

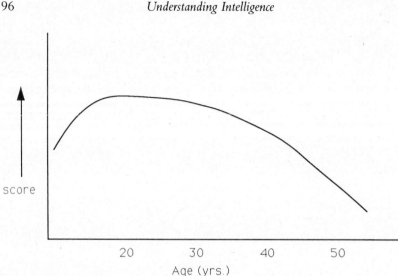

Figure 5.2   Typical rise and fall of IQ test scores with age

Again, the 'development' we see is an artefact of the way the tests are constructed to correlate with school performance over the school years.

Stability or consistency of IQ at different ages

As we have already seen several times, IQ is not so much a measure as a *ranking*
of subjects' responses on a scale of items as reflecting what? No one is very sure,
except that it is usually presumed to reflect some underlying mental strength or
power. Thus when we use IQ for purposes of studying development, all we are
really doing is seeing how this ranking changes from age to age. When the IQs
of a group of children are taken and then retested at a later age, the correlation
between scores typically decreases as the age gap increases. This has been a
regular finding in the growth studies (see Bayley 1970 for review). It has been
the subject of some debate concerning the 'changeability' of IQ.

Recent debate around these issues makes the problems of the approach very
clear. The first issue at stake is the empirical matter of whether mature intellectual status can be *predicted* from mental measures obtained at a very early age.
The second issue is the important theoretical matter about whether development can be considered to be to some extent simply a process of growth or
maturation of a discrete or unitary entity (in which case the same entity is being
measured at two different ages and correlations should be appreciable); or
whether development really does consist of continual change and reconstruc-
tion (in which case what is being examined at two different ages is quite
different). The research strategy accordingly has been to seek correlations between test scores at different ages.

The first problem, of course, is that of knowing what to test, and how to test it, at different ages. Typically tests of one sort have been given in infancy and other tests at a later age, according to what 'is available' for measurement, rather than any theoretical developmental rationale. This has presented huge problems of interpretation. As Bornstein and Sigman (1986) complain, most of the tests given in infancy are not tests of 'cognitive' abilities, but of simple motor and sensory abilities such as reaching, grasping and general orientation. The latter 'bear little conceptual relation to measures included in traditional psychometric tests of intelligence administered in childhood' (1986: 252). What we should be seeking, according to these authors, are correlations based on 'information-processing skills' and measures. More recently two measures of such skills have been proposed, and 'both have been found to show moderate but significant levels of continuity with measures of cognitive competence in childhood' (1986: 252).

What are these measures and what can we make of such results? The two measures involve the infants' duration of attention to stimuli presented in a laboratory setting. Infants as young as 2 months are placed in a baby chair in front of a screen on which a picture of an object or pattern is presented. The infant will usually examine the picture for a period and then cease to look, or 'habituate', and the length of this period decreases with repeated presentations. The total amount of time spent looking at the stimulus (either in a single or over repeated presentations) is called the 'total fixation time' or 'time to habituation'. The assumption is that this measure reflects the efficiency of information processing in the infants' brain: the more time an infant spends looking at the same stimulus, the less efficient his or her information-processing apparatus is supposed to be. Conversely if a novel stimulus is then presented, the amount of time the infant spends looking at it, relative to the 'old' stimulus – 'novelty preference' or 'response to novelty' – is also considered to reflect the efficiency of information-processing (Bornstein and Sigman 1986).

Bornstein and Sigman review several studies which indicate that these measures correlate with other indices of mental activity in children, including problem-solving, exploration of their environments, and complexity of play. More to the point, several studies have shown that the measures of decrement and recovery of attention taken in the first six months of life correlate moderately but significantly (i.e. around 0.5) with psychometric test scores taken between 2 and 8 years of age:

> We calculated that decrement in infancy and cognition in childhood share 15 per cent of common variance, that recovery and cognition share 22 per cent, and that the overall common variance shared by the infancy and childhood measures was 18 per cent.
>
> (Bornstein and Sigman 1986: 256)

These may not sound like big values but Bornstein and Sigman make several points. First, they insist that the measures of attention genuinely reflect central control systems or capacities that vary across individuals. Then, to explain the continuity implied in the correlations, they propose three possibilities:

1 continuity of identical behavior
2 continuity of underlying process
3 continuity of developmental status.

Since quite different measures are used the first possibility is not really an option. The second possibility might be, although the infancy measures correlate differently with different subscores in childhood – e.g. with 'verbal intelligence' but not with recognition memory or discrimination learning – so that a 'general intelligence' is unlikely to be the underlying process.

Bornstein and Sigman favour 'mental representation' as a more specific 'underlying process' linking the two measures: the rate of decrement or recovery of attention in childhood might be a reflection of 'representation formation', they suggest; test scores in childhood might reflect the same ability: hence the correlation. The investigators are cautious about this possibility, though, because 'We can only speculate about the nature of representation in the mental life of the infant' (1986: 262). On the other hand, they suggest, the measures could correlate through more peripheral processes such as motivation or self-regulation. The third possibility in the list above is a more open question because it assumes equivalent status on two different measures that is not merely coincidental, but linked by some as yet unspecified causes.

Bornstein and Sigman rightly note a fourth possibility: that the age-to-age correlation could be a spurious one, in that it arises from a mediating variable that is non-cognitive or non-intellectual. Assuming that the continuity is genuine, however, how does it arise and become maintained? Bornstein and Sigman note that simply to attribute the individual differences concerned to genetics would be extremely difficult to confirm (note that the continuity implies identical *developmental* programmes in different individuals, but, by virtue of different genes, different starting- and end-points). On the other hand different familial experiences, such as rearing styles that could account for individual differences in attention, have been well documented. For example coarticulation of mother's with infant's behaviour, parents' responsivity to infants' habituation, the frequency with which parents attract infants' attention to objects and events, and amount of social interaction, all are correlated with habituation times in infants.

These could be related to developmental continuity either by direct effect on the maturation of a 'central control process' (intelligence) which maintains a 'good start' through to test several years later. Or it could be the basis of a spurious correlation in that the (parental/familial forces) which create an advantage in the test situation at, say, 3 months, are also effective in the test situation at, say, 6 years. Bornstein and Sigman cite much evidence to suggest that these forces do actually persist over this age span. Overall, however, 'we can conclude very little about the origins and maintenance of individual differences in infant cognitive functioning beyond what logic dictates' (1986: 265).

We have gone into this study in some detail because it illustrates the many difficulties in studying development from a psychometric point of view. Because it involves a description of individual differences rather than of the trait itself, and also viewing a test score as a trait score, we arrive at several difficulties:

1 the ubiquitous difficulties of interpretation in correlational studies
2 the fact that test scores aren't giving any absolute measure of development status, only status with respect to a population of peers
3 even accepting the correlation as causal we arrive at a curious conundrum: if it endures, then the process being observed is maturational; if it does not, then the process is probably developmental. In other words, if we can 'see' a correlation across ages, the process is non-developmental (merely maturational); if it is developmental we wouldn't be able to 'see' it as a correlation.

Even highly meticulous and circumspect studies have difficulty in describing development in this way; all that can be described, in fact, is change or continuity in measurement status relative to a subject's peers. By such means we are not describing the development of intelligence, only the changes with age of a surrogate. This is not uninteresting but it is not development. Describing population changes or continuities is not the same thing as describing development of the trait or character as it develops in any member of the species.

The phrase 'continuity in development' is, in fact, almost a contradiction in terms. But this is the kind of contradiction the psychometric approach forces us to accept. Because we are only describing changes in an index relative to peers we are never sure what they are changes or continuities *in*. We can hypothesise of course, but often many new assumptions have to be continually brought in to make these sound plausible. Thus it is common to find almost any measurable trait (attention, motivation, self-regulation, etc.) taken on board as 'intelligence' if it makes a hypothesis sound plausible. The cost in terms of loss of precision (and therefore testability) is obvious.

We may quibble, of course, about other forms of simplification (such as the belief that 'habituation time' equals 'efficiency of information processing' which, again, is an assumption which has no evidence to support it; or the claim that test scores equals 'cognition in childhood') but these are less important than the general strategic difficulties already mentioned. These difficulties largely stem from adherence to a view of intelligence as an underlying mental strength or power, the relative 'quantity' of which, in any individual, changes little with age.

Development in information processing

Instead of viewing intelligence *simply* as a unitary power, the information-processing approach attempts to characterise it in terms of cognitive processes or components (as we saw in Chapter 3). The developmental problem is then one of describing how these and their interactions change with age. Sternberg (1988) reviews research concerning several possible strands of development in intelligence:

1 the development of control strategies such as monitoring, chunking of information, and selectivity of responses in problem-solving
2 increase in the sheer amount of information that can be processed by the individual
3 ability to analyse increasingly complex, or 'higher order' relations (as in analogies between analogies)
4 increase in flexibility of thinking.

All of these possibilities are supported in the research at a descriptive level, i.e. they increase with age. But no clear *developmental* theory has yet emerged from the diverse findings. In consequence the literature is, once again, dominated by *ad hoc* accounts. Of course, we must not forget the enormous difficulty of constructing theory in this domain.

Other information-processing theories have been based on the notions of growth or development in both processing resources and processing efficiency (see Kail and Bisanz 1982; Kail and Pellegrino 1985 for reviews). Perhaps the best known example of the former type is Pascual-Leone's (1970) theory, which posits cognitive development in terms of increase in size of a 'central computing space'. Case (1985) incorporates a similar idea in his theory of development. Theories of the second type are based on the frequent observation that as children get older they tend to use more complex rules or strategies of reasoning or knowledge management. For example, they use more efficient and more productive computational strategies in simple arithmetic (Kail and Pellegrino 1985). They are capable of using more complex rules in problem-solving (Seigler 1983). And they may be said to construct more complex 'mental models', and better *procedures* for constructing and testing them with age (Johnson-Laird *et al.* 1986; Oakhill 1988).

These are also extremely interesting ideas that are revealing what sort of cognitive competencies children have at different ages. The very diversity of formulation, however, suggests that they still have an *ad hoc* character: although they may be helping to identify *what* changes in the course of development, the *how* of development remains a more distant goal. In tracing changes in intelligence to changes in cognitive characteristics, rather than to a simple underlying strength or power, however, such studies reflect the strategy of investigation of Jean Piaget and others. We shall consider some of the fruits of this less mechanistic, more 'organic', approach in the rest of this chapter.

Piaget

To Piaget, intelligence is the whole system of cognitive adaptation in humans; intelligence consists of knowledge and the cognitive functions integral to the form of knowledge representation. This entails a theory of knowledge known as 'constructivism', which distinguishes it from 'rationalism' (the theory that knowledge is innate) and 'associationism' (the theory that knowledge consists of passive registration of associations in the world). The development of intelligence, according to this theory, consists of

> The establishment of cognitive or, more generally, epistemological relations, which consist neither of a simple copy of external objects nor of a mere unfolding of structures preformed inside the subject, but rather involve a set of structures progressively constructed by continuous interaction between the subject and the external world.
>
> (Piaget 1970: 703)

A theory of the development of intelligence thus consists of a general description of the course of development together with the principles which govern its particular expressions at a certain level of development, or in a certain individual. To Piaget these bear close analogy with principles governing biological adaptation in the development of other organs and other organisms. Two processes in particular implement adaptation. One of these is assimilation, the process by which external elements are integrated into an existing structure: 'no behaviour, even if it is new to the individual, constitutes an absolute beginning. It is always grafted onto previous schemes and therefore amounts to assimilating new elements to already constructed structures' (Piaget 1970: 704). As illustration Piaget considers the 'sucking' schema of the infant. At first this is confined to only one external element, the mother's breast. But later, other elements such as the thumb or other objects become assimilated to the sucking schema.

Such assimilation, however, always involves an adjustment to the mental schema or structure; Piaget calls this accommodation. The other objects sucked, for instance, vary in shape and size and require compensatory adjustments to the shape of the mouth and lips, and so on. These adjustments become part of the now extended sucking schema. This equilibrium between assimilation and accommodation is what Piaget saw as the essence of cognitive adaptation, and in various forms 'drives' the course of development and the construction of intelligence. 'In the development of intelligence in the child, there are many types of equilibrium between assimilation and accommodation that vary with the levels of development and the problem to be solved' (Piaget 1970: 712).

These different types of equilibrium, and the structure they involve, in time give rise to and define the various stages of development in Piaget's theory. What develops, according to Piaget, is the integration of schemes into more inclusive structures. These integrations result in well-defined levels or stages of development, because they give rise to characteristic mental abilities and behaviours. Each succeeding stage builds upon the one before it to constitute a necessary, universal sequence: 'cognitive stages have a sequential property, that is, they appear in a fixed order of succession because each one of them is necessary for the formation of the following one' (Piaget 1970: 714). The stages are sensorimotor intelligence, pre-operational, concrete operational and formal operational intelligence.

Sensorimotor intelligence

Development builds on to pre-existing structures. The infant enters the world with structures we call reflexes: grasping, sucking, blinking, and so on. The development of intelligence starts with the modification of these structures through the processes of assimilation and accommodation just described. We have already mentioned how the sucking reflex becomes modified in this way. Similarly with the grasping reflex: it becomes modified by grasping a vast range of articles of different shapes, sizes, textures, and so on, over and over again. In each of these there is an action (a sequence of muscle contractions) and there is an 'effect' consisting of sensations in the muscles, joints and tendons as they move, and those caused by the weight and shape of the object as it 'stretches' the tendons, etc., and deforms the tissues with which it comes into contact; and also those of *affect* or feelings (pleasure, joy or whatever). The function of a structure is to 'co-ordinate' these internal and external sensations and actions. We see it in operation when a child reaches for an object, say, with the shape of the hand already anticipating the shape and weight of the object.

These direct co-ordinations of actions and sensations which dominate the first four months of life begin to change thereafter. First, objects that are grasped may be used to produce a *secondary* effect, such as a rattle being grasped and then shaken to produce a noise. The different schemes may themselves become co-ordinated, as when an object is first grasped and then brought up the mouth to be sucked; or when a cloth on which an object rests may be pulled in order to gain access to the object which is then grasped. Through the co-ordination of external sensations emanating from objects, the 'sensations of action' in muscles and joints, and the internal sensations *resulting* from action, the child begins to differentiate internal from external space, and the body and its properties from other objects and *their* properties.

The 'co-ordination of co-ordinations' furnishes important intellectual advances. For example attributes of objects that aren't immediately obvious can be predicted – such as its location from the manner of its disappearance. The consequences of events and actions can be anticipated, and compensated for, in advance of the action itself. Events, such as the sound produced by a parent, can be imitated even though the child cannot 'see' his or her own mouth or larynx in the process, and may never, in fact, have made such a sound before. In such cases the child must rely instead on translation from a purely internal representation. Finally, the child of about 18 months can use these representations in the absence of the objects and actions they represent: surrogate objects are used in play; and the child can communicate reference to objects and actions in the form of words. This capacity for 'symbolic operations' signals the end of the sensorimotor period and the advent of the pre-operational period.

Pre-operational intelligence

The conspicuous feature of this level of co-ordination of structures is that the structures can be '*re*-presented' by signifiers (images, words and other symbols) which are differentiated from what they signify (the significates). These symbols are then operated upon to 'think' actions and events in the absence of the significates. Thus the co-ordinations among the concrete stimuli of the world and the child's actions upon them are now internalised.

This furnishes many new powers, as just pointed out; but these are still incomplete. According to Piaget, this is seen in many idiosyncrasies of thought at this stage. Because action is usually one-directional, so is the child's thinking at this stage; the child's thought is said to lack reversibility. The evidence which Piaget evoked in support of this conclusion comes from some of his most famous 'conservation' experiments, in which the act of transforming the arrangement of some substance or array of objects also appears to be interpreted by the child as an indelible transformation on its length, weight, or whatever (see Figure 4.2 and discussion of conservation in Chapter 4).

In this stage, then, the child's thinking is said to be still stimulus-bound, so that visual perception dominates thinking. In particular, there is inadequate co-ordination between variables in representation so that the child fails to realise that the increase in one dimension (the length of the clay ball, say) is compensated for by a decrease in another (the thickness). Piaget called this lack of circumspection 'centration'. It is particularly evident, according to Piaget, in the way that children under about 7 years fail to adopt another person's point of view in certain situations: they are said to be 'egocentric'.

In spite of these inadequacies, the pre-operational period is a time of advance and preparation: advance in the sense that internalisation of actions has taken place; and preparation for the new construction in the period of concrete operations, which follows at around 7–8 years.

Concrete operational intelligence (7–11 years)

As the term implies, children with operational intelligence have certain operations at their disposal. These are evident in certain powers which include reversibility, decentration and nonegocentrism. Just as the construction of sensorimotor intelligence entailed the co-ordination of stimuli and actions, these now become fully co-ordinated *in thought*. Thus compensation among variables becomes evident in conservation tasks; thought can be detached, or decentred, from a particular aspect or variable so that alternative points of view can be appreciated. Also certain logical relations become available to the child.

A major characteristic of this period, however, is that the child's thinking is still concerned with concrete stimuli and concrete actions: hence the full title given this period. The child with sensorimotor intelligence can do things with objects, and the concrete operational child can *think* about doing those things. But the latter cannot think about propositions and relations detached from particular objects and events. This entails another period of development.

Formal operational intelligence (11 years to adult)

On the basis of equilibrations which take place in the concrete operational period a new level of mental construction emerges, according to Piaget, after the age of 11–12 years to form fully adult and 'scientific' intelligence. The operations tied to objects and events in the previous period are now brought together under a single coherent system of thought. These allow thought which is abstract and mathematical, logical and circumspect. Thus the child in this stage can entertain premises that are only hypothetical, can deduce consequences arising from these premises, and thus know how to put hypotheses to the test. In the process of testing the child will appreciate the value of keeping some variables constant while others are being manipulated.

As evidence of this new construction Piaget invoked the results of several tasks given before and during this period. For example children of 10 years or under have great difficulty with the following task:

John is shorter than Bill
John is taller than Fred
Who is the tallest?

Children with formal operational intelligence, however, have little difficulty with it.

In another task, children were given a variety of objects (and a bucket of water) and had to classify the objects according to whether or not they floated on water. That done, they were then asked to use the same apparatus to explain the basis of the classification.

As Inhelder and Piaget (1958) point out, the solution to this task requires the existence not only of certain operations at the concrete level, such as the conservation of weight, but also of other, more abstract, relations that become available only as formal operations. These include the relation between weight and volume (i.e. density) and the relation between the density of an object and the density of an equivalent volume of water (i.e. its specific gravity).

In another task, children were presented with four bottles of colourless liquid and a dropper in a bottle. The latter (labelled 'g') contains potassium iodine; the flasks contain (a) dilute sulphuric acid; (b) water; (c) oxygenated water; (d) thiosulphate. The subjects were asked to combine the liquids in order to produce a yellow colour. The correct combination is the dilute sulphuric acid, the oxygenated water and the potassium iodine: $a+c+g$. The following responses by children of different ages illustrate the advent of formal operations (Inhelder and Piaget 1958).

1 *Pre-operational intelligence (5–6 years)*   The child randomly associates two chemicals at a time and makes no attempt at causal explanation.
2 *Early concrete operational intelligence (7–8 years)*   Subjects tend to combine each chemical separately with the contents of the bottle; no further combinations are attempted without specific suggestion from the experimenter.
3 *Late concrete operational intelligence (9–11 years)*   Subjects tend to continue as in the previous stage but sometimes combine the products of each trial (e.g. $(a+g) + (c+g)$).
4 *Early formal operational intelligence (12–13 years)*   Subjects now tend to combine three chemicals at a time, and sometimes keep a record of their trials, although these still tend to be random.
5 *Late formal operational intelligence (14–15 years)*   Subjects organise a systematic series of tests; keep a record of trials as they go through; continue to exhaust all possibilities even if they have already found a combination that 'works'; and construct new tests to test their conclusions further.

With the advent of this system, knowledge itself becomes a resource for the construction of *further* knowledge, and we have a fully operational human intelligence.

Evaluation and criticism of Piaget's theory

Contemporary views of Piaget's theory are very mixed. Perhaps a summary might take the form, 'there are many problems about the theory, but there's a great deal to be said for it'. As Meadows (1988) put it:

> Much of what he said was wrong, some misleading. There are many gaps in the work – but who can be expected to deal with *every* aspect of complex issues? Still, his contribution over a wide range of matter and over a long period of years has been enormous.
>
> (Meadows 1988: 19)

Evaluation and criticism revolve around three important questions. First, how does the general approach to understanding intelligence compare with others? Second, are the core concepts and relations of the theory reasonably clear and coherent? Third, does the theory provide an accurate description of the development of intelligence and of the principles governing it? Finally, some theorists have been concerned about serious omissions in the theory. We shall describe each of these points of criticism in turn.

Piaget's approach to intelligence
Above all else Piaget was concerned with a comprehensive theory of intelligence rather than with utilitarian, piecemeal accounts. The latter may be

useful for particular, restricted, purposes but affords us no general understanding. This was the point made by Montangero (1985) – whom we quoted in Chapter 3 – in comparing the Piagetian with the information-processing (largely American) approaches concerned with the intelligence involved in specific tasks:

> This particularity as well as the everlasting tendency to define intelligence by the tasks achieved rather than by its structural or procedural characteristics is in accordance with the pragmatic character of the American mind. In the United States psychology tends to focus on what is useful and efficient. It is why it looks for operational constructs rather than for comprehensive theories.
>
> (Montangero 1985: 98–9)

Piaget's theory presupposes intelligence to be a 'systemic' character, rather than an isolable trait such as 'judgement' or the 'eduction of correlates' or 'speed of processing'. This global quality of intelligence as seen by Piaget can hardly be overestimated: 'intelligence constitutes the state of equilibrium to which tend all the successive adaptations of a sensorimotor and cognitive nature, as well as all assimilatory and accommodatory interactions between the organism and the environment' (Piaget 1947: 11; quoted by Dasen 1984).

Piaget's theory is also 'organic', in contrast with the mechanistic approaches of the information-processing school, discussed earlier. For example, the theory depicts representations and operations as inextricably tied together, in contrast with the separation of 'processes' from the 'knowledge base' in the information-processing approaches.

And of course, in Piaget's view, *par excellence*, intelligence is something that develops through a process of change, involving the active responses of the individual, rather than an entity which ineluctably matures, as in the psychometric approach.

Core components and relations

As we saw in Chapter 1, a good theory must describe the components of the system being described as clearly as possible; a theory of the *development* of this system must also describe how these components change, possibly into something quite different, over time. There are problems in the way that Piaget described the key components of development (assimilation, accommodation and equilibration). Most authors accept that these are suitable *analogies* of the processes. But there are many uncertainties about how they actually work. Piaget spoke of a kind of innate 'drive to assimilate': 'any scheme of assimilation tends to feed itself, that is to incorporate outside elements compatible with its nature in to itself' (Piaget 1978: 7; quoted by Meadows 1987). But there is much that remains to be specified in this process: what counts as an element or experience? What decides compatibility? How does the 'feeding' occur? How do we know whether a given experience is going to be assimilated by a particular child? Without more material description the theory is in danger of being idealistic. The same reservations can be made about the concepts of accommodation and equilibration.

This vagueness is also evident when we turn to the *products* of development, the structures and operations of reasoning. Again, Piaget used analogies to describe these: namely the laws of formal or propositional logic. And he some-times seemed to be claiming an identity between them: 'reasoning is nothing more than the propositional calculus itself' (Inhelder and Piaget 1958: 305). Many authors in recent years have railed against this idea as a suitable descrip-tion of intelligence. We described in the previous chapter the doubts arising about the existence of laws or rules of logic separate from *particular* knowledge or contexts. Johnson-Laird (1983) described this tendency as a flaw which runs through Piaget's theory 'like a geological fault'.

Apart from the fact that Piaget's accounts of propositional logic have been found to contain mathematical or logical errors, the notion of logical structures has thus been found to be vague and difficult to operationalise (Case 1985). There have, accordingly, been several attempts to revise the theory by recasting parts of it in different terms, largely those of contemporary information-processing psychology (as we saw in the previous section). It is too early to tell whether these have achieved durable improvements.

Empirical problems

Probably the first difficulty in assessing this question is the uniqueness of Piaget's methods. Piaget and his co-workers used a 'clinical method' involving the close monitoring of children's responses to tasks and questions usually accompanied by much *ad hoc* subsidiary questioning and manipulation. The conditions of investigation were not rigorously controlled and there has been much debate about whether the method can be called truly scientific. Also Piaget's descriptions of apparatus, subjects and procedures was often rather vague, which has made replication of the studies very difficult.

Empirically too, although there have been numerous replications of Piaget's basic findings, even in diverse cultural settings (Dasen 1984), only slight modi-fications of procedure have produced quite different results and, consequently, quite different interpretations. One of the most famous is the experiment by McGarrigle and Donaldson(1974) (described in Chapter 4) in which a 'naughty teddy' rearranged the conservation test materials. Given such 'human sense' the problem became soluble to a majority of children who had previously 'failed' it (see also Donaldson 1978). Other conflicting findings have emerged in areas like classification of objects in which young children seem to display abilities that Piaget claims are theoretically impossible (e.g. Markman *et al.* 1981; Scott *et al.* 1985; Bauer and Mandler 1989).

In the domain of formal reasoning there are similar criticisms of Piaget's description of intelligence. Children in the prior stage may be 'failing' the tasks for trivial, task-structural reasons, rather than cognitive-structural reasons

(Wollman 1982); and the apparent attainment of formal operational intelligence appears to be school-related (Dasen 1984). Even in well-schooled cultures, however, formal operational intelligence as described by Piaget is often not evident. King (1985), for example, reviewed twenty-five large-scale investigations, and concluded:

> A sizable proportion of the normal adult population does not reason at formal levels when tested on formal operations tasks. The rates of successful performance (i.e. scoring at the fully formal level) averaged 40–70 per cent for the college students and adults tested in these samples. . . . These data are clearly a challenge to the assumption of the universality of attainment of the formal operations level.
>
> (King 1985: 15)

There is considerable uncertainty at the present time about whether Piaget's theory provides an accurate account of the development of intelligence, and of the principles governing it.

What is left out?

Finally, more recent authors have pointed to a major omission in Piaget's theory, namely the social context in which the intelligence of all humans develops. Piaget (e.g. 1932) seems to have been sensitive to these issues in his earlier writings, but such interest became increasingly sporadic as he pursued the structural aspects of intelligence in the idealistic individual. So, as Bruner (1985: 26) put it, 'in the Piagetian model . . . a lone child struggles single-handed to strike some equilibrium between assimilating the world to himself or himself to the world'. Over the last decade or so theorists have sought more realistic, social, foundations of the development of intelligence and have found them in the 'socio-historical' theories which we mentioned in Chapter 4. We shall now attempt to summarise these.

Development of intelligence as socio-history

We saw in Chapter 4 how much of the theorising in this field stems from the writings of L.S. Vygotsky. It may be remembered how Vygotsky saw the whole basis of human thought and intelligence in the social, productive processes of people, mediated by 'tools' of various kinds: 'the very mechanism underlying higher mental functions is a copy from social interaction; all higher mental functions are internalised social relationships' (Vygotsky 1981: 161). Development thus consists of the progressive internalisation, mentally, of these external 'cultural tools'. Vygotsky formulated this as the 'general genetic law of cultural development':

> Any function in the child's cultural development appears twice, or on two planes. First it appears on the social plane, and then on the

psychological plane. First it appears between people as an inter-psychological category, and then within the child as an intrapsychological category. This is equally true with regard to voluntary attention, logical memory, the formation of concepts, and the development of volition.

(Vygotsky 1981: 163)

At the heart of the developmental process is what Vygotsky called 'internalization'. As children first begin to use cultural tools (e.g. calculating and communicating tools, traffic rules and folk rituals) their mental processes are directed through these to other people they are invariably being used with. The mental functions of the young child are thus mediated from without before they become used 'from within'. Vygotsky 'referred to this entire process as the complete circle of cultural-historical development of mental functions in ontogenesis' (Davydov and Radzikhovskii 1985: 54).

But the course of this development was not seen as the simple process of replicating mentally, or reducing the mind to, the external processes themselves. 'He did not recognise determination [of mental processes] as a simple reduction of mind to labour activity' (Davydov and Radzikhovskii 1985: 63). Rather there is a dialectical relation between the 'inside' and the 'outside', involving cognitive conflict and frequent reorganisation of the 'inside', just as the 'outside' has frequently been reorganised in human history.

> Our concept of development implies a rejection of the frequently held view that cognitive development results from the gradual accumulation of separate changes. We believe that child development is a complex dialectical process characterized by periodicity, unevenness in the development of different functions, metamorphoses or qualititative transformation of one form into another, intertwining of internal and external factors, and adaptive processes which overcome impediments that the child encounters.
>
> (Vygotsky 1978: 7)

It is not a simple process because it entails a meeting between the mature forms of thought and behaviour encountered socially and the more primitive forms in the child. In the course of this meeting, new forms appear, 'which does not simply involve a stereotyped reproduction of chains formed in advance' (Vygotsky 1988/1989: 65). Rather there is creative adaptation.

Vygotsky (e.g. 1981) complained about the tendency to pose the problem of intellectual development purely in quantitative terms, and also about the corollary of this tendency, the 'negative characterization of the child' which 'methods tell us about what the child does not have or what is lacking in the child compared with the adult' (1981: 63). Thus Vygotsky saw the emergence of wholly new species in phylogeny as a better analogy of intellectual development than Piaget's analogy of embryogenesis.

Much attention has recently been drawn to what Vygotsky saw as the

dialectical relation between the mature and the immature intellects in development; in particular, to what he called the 'zone of proximal development'
(ZPD). It is worth looking at this idea fairly closely because it clarifies further
this notion of the social bases of the intellectual development. To use
Vygotsky's words, the zone of proximal development is 'the distance between
the actual developmental level as determined by independent problem solving
and the level of potential development as determined through problem solving
under the guidance or in collaboration with more capable peers' (Vygotsky
1978: 86). The ZPD is thus a domain of interaction in which an adult or expert
supports in various ways the problem-solving of the child or novice, thus
ensuring an intellectual advance that would not otherwise have occurred.

The processes in the ZPD have been illustrated in many studies. Wood *et al.*
(1976) for instance observed 3–5-year-olds being tutored in building pyramids
out of interlocking wooden blocks. Bruner (1985) describes the characteristic
strategy of the tutor in such situations as follows.

> First is to model the task, to establish that something is possible and
> interesting. In this case, it consists of constructing the pyramid slowly,
> with conspicuous marking of the subassemblies that the child will need
> later. The child, somehow, is induced to try. . . . It is very obscure how
> an adult gets a child to venture into the zone. . . . It relates to minimizing
> the cost, indeed the possibility, of error. Once the child is willing to try,
> the tutor's general task is that of scaffolding – reducing the number of
> degrees of freedom that the child must manage in the task. She does it by
> segmenting the task and ritualizing it: creating a format, a nanocosm . . .
> she sees to it that the child does only what he can do and then she fills in
> the rest – as in slipping the pegs of certain blocks into the holes of others
> to which they are mated, the child having brought them next to each
> other. She limits the complexity of the task to the level that the child can
> just manage.
>
> (Bruner 1985: 29–30)

This characteristic mode of learning and teaching the culture has been demonstrated in many areas, especially in the highly complex domain of first language
learning where young children develop with enormous speed (see e.g. Bruner
1983). In such ways, children rapidly become intelligent in communication
and thoughts and actions which are embedded in social formats. This explains
why children may appear to be – and are frequently assessed to be – 'un-
intelligent' in strange learning situations. As Bruner (1985) puts it:

> The fact that we learn the culture as readily and effectively as we do must
> give us pause – considering how poorly we do at certain artificial,
> 'madeup' subjects that we teach in schools and whose use is *not* imbedded
> in any established cultural practice.
>
> (Bruner 1985: 29)

Again, however, we have to stress that this development is not a process in which the child is a passive recipient of 'intelligence'. The child brings to the ZPD the intelligence he or she already has, so that the result is a combination of this with whatever is presented under the guidance of the tutor. There is much scope for individual, as opposed to stereotyped, adaptations in this zone where culture and cognition meet (Cole 1985). As Rogoff (1989) claims, children 'do not simply receive the guidance of adults, they seek, structure, and even demand the assistance of those around them in learning how to solve problems of all kinds' (1989: 58).

It is for these reasons that Newman *et al.* (1989) argue for a view of individual cognition and interpersonal processes as a single 'functional system'. The direction of individual development, according to them, is determined by interactions in the ZPD: what is initially inter-psychological subsequently becomes intra-psychological (an illustration of this, the case of an 'intersection schema' for combining pairs of chemicals, was provided in Chapter 4). But, because the process is socio-historical rather than individual (as in Piaget's theory), the resulting cognitive constructions are more creative and more variable.

References

Ausubel, D.P. and Sullivan, E.V. (1970). *Theory and Problems of Child Development*. New York, Grune & Stratton.

Bauer, P.J. and Mandler, J.M. (1989). Taxonomies and triads: conceptual organisation in one- to two-year-olds. *Cognitive Psychology*, 21: 156–84.

Bayley, N. (1970). Development of mental abilities. In P.H. Mussen (ed.) *Manual of Child Psychology*. London, Wiley.

Bornstein, M.H. and Sigman, M.D. (1986). Continuity in mental development from infancy. *Child Development*, 57: 251–74.

Bruner, J.S. (1983). *Child's Talk*. Oxford, Oxford University Press.

—— (1985). Vygotsky: a historical and conceptual perspective. In J.V. Wertsch (ed.) *Culture, Communication and Cognition: Vygotskian Perspectives*. Cambridge, Cambridge University Press.

Butcher, H. (1968). *Human Intelligence*. London, Methuen.

Case, R. (1985). *Intellectual Development: Birth to Adulthood*. New York, Academic Press.

Cattell, R.B. (1971). *Abilities: Their Structures, Growth and Action*. Boston, Mass., Houghton Mifflin.

Cole, M. (1985). The zone of proximal development: where culture and cognition create each other. In J.V. Wertsch (ed.) Culture, Communication and Cognition: Vygotskian Perspectives. Cambridge, Cambridge University Press.

Dasen, P.R. (1984). The cross-cultural study of intelligence: Piaget and the Baoule. In P. Fry (ed.) *Changing Conceptions of Intelligence and Intellectual Functioning*. Amsterdam, North-Holland.

Davidov, V.V. and Radzikhovskii, L.A. (1989). In J.V. Wertsch (ed.) *Culture, Communication and Cognition: Vygotskian Perspectives*. Cambridge, Cambridge University Press.

Donaldson, M. (1978). *Children's Minds*. London, Fontana.

Garcia, J. (1972). IQ: The conspiracy. *Psychology Today*, September: 14–22.

Horn, J.L. (1982). The ageing of human abilities. In B.B. Wolman (ed.) *Handbook of Developmental Psychology*. Englewood Cliffs, NJ, Prentice-Hall.

Inhelder, B. and Piaget, J. (1958). *The Growth of Logical Thinking: From Childhood to Adolescence*. New York, Basic Books.

—— (1964). *The Early Growth of Logic in the Child: Classification and Seriation*. London, Routledge & Kegan Paul.

Johnson-Laird, P.N. (1983). *Mental Models*. Cambridge, Cambridge University Press.

Johnson-Laird, P.N., Oakhill, J.V. and Bull, D. (1986). Children's syllogistic reasoning. *Quarterly Journal of Experimental Psychology*, 38A: 35–58.

Kail, R. and Bisanz, J. (1982). Information processing and cognitive development. In H.W. Reese (ed.) *Advances in Child Development and Behaviour*, vol. 17. New York, Academic Press.

Kail, R. and Pellegrino, J.W. (1985). *Human Intelligence: Perspectives and Prospects*. New York, Freeman.

King, P.M. (1985). Formal reasoning in adults: a review and critique. In R.A. Mines and K.S. Kitchener (eds) *Adult Cognitive Development*. New York, Praeger.

Kuhn, D. (1988). Cognitive development. In M.H. Bornstein and M.E. Lamb (eds) *Developmental Psychology: An Advanced Textbook*, 2nd edn. Hillsdale, NJ, Erlbaum.

McGarrigle, J. and Donaldson, M. (1974). Conservation accidents. *Cognition*, 3: 341–50.

Markman, E., Cox, B. and Machida, S. (1981). The standard object-sorting task as a measure of conceptual organisation. *Developmental Psychology*, 17: 115–17.

Meadows, S. (1988). Piaget's contribution to understanding cognitive development: an assessment for the late 1980s. In K. Richardson and S. Sheldon (eds) *Cognitive Development to Adolescence*. Hove, Erlbaum.

Montangero, J. (1985). *Genetic Epistemology: Yesterday and Today*. New York, The Graduate School and University Centre.

Newman, D., Griffin, P. and Cole, M. (1989). *The Construction Zone: Working for Cognitive Change in School*. Cambridge, Cambridge University Press.

Oakhill, J. (1988). The development of reasoning ability: information-processing approaches. In K. Richardson and S. Sheldon (eds) *Cognitive Development to Adolescence*. Hove, Erlbaum.

Pascual-Leone, J. (1970 A mathematical model for the transition rule in Piaget's developmental stages. *Acta Psychologica*: 32: 301–45.

Piaget, J. (1932). *The Moral Judgement of the Child*. London, Routledge & Kegan Paul.

—— (1947/1950). *The Psychology of Intelligence*. London, Routledge & Kegan Paul.

—— (1957). *Logic and Psychology*. New York, Basic Books.

—— (1970). Piaget's theory. In P.H. Mussen (ed.) *Manual of Child Psychology*. London, Wiley.

—— (1978). *The Development of Thought: Equilibration of Cognitive Structures*. Oxford: Basil Blackwell.

Rogoff, B. (1989). The joint socialization of development by young children and adults. In A. Gellatly, D. Rogers and J.A. Sloboda (eds) *Cognition and Social Worlds*. Oxford, Clarendon.

Schaie, K. and Herzog, K.W. (1986). Towards a comprehensive model of adult intellectual development: contributions to the Seattle Longitudinal Study. In R.J.

Sternberg (ed.) *Advances in the Psychology of Human Intelligence*, Vol. 3. Hillsdale, NJ. Erlbaum.

Scott, M.S., Greenfield, D.B. and Urbano, R. (1985). A comparison of complimentary and taxonomic organisation: effects of the dependent measure. *International Journal of Behavioural Development*, 8, 241–56.

Siegler, R.S. (1976). Three aspects of cognitive development. *Cognitive Psychology*, 8: 481–520.

—— (1983). Information processing approaches to development. In P.H. Mussen (ed.) *Handbook of Child Psychology*, vol. 1, 4th edn. Hillsdale, NJ, Erlbaum.

Seitz, V. (1988). Methodology. In M.H. Bornstein and M.E.Lamb (eds) *Developmental Psychology: An Advanced Textbook*, 2nd ed. Hillsdale, NJ, Erlbaum.

Smith, J., Dixon, R.A. and Baltes, P.B. (1988). Expertise in life-planning: a new research approach to investigating aspects of wisdom. In M.L. Commons, J.D. Swift, F.A. Richards and C. Armou (eds.) *Advances in Development VI: Comparisons and Applications of Development Models*. New York, Praeger.

Sternberg, R.J. (1988). Intellectual development: Psychometric and information-processing approaches. In M.H. Bornstein and M.E. Lamb (eds) *Developmental Psychology: An Advanced Textbook*, 2nd edn. Hillsdale, NJ, Erlbaum.

Verster, J.M. (1987). Human cognition and intelligence: towards an integrated theoretical perspective. In S.H. Irvine and S.E. Newstead (eds) *Intelligence and Cognition: Contemporary Frames of Reference*. Dordrecht, Martinus Nijhoff.

Vygotsky, L.S. (1978). *Mind in Society*. Cambridge, Mass., Harvard University Press.

—— (1981). The genesis of higher mental functions. In J.V. Wertsch (ed.) *The Concept of Activity in Soviet Psychology*. New York, Sharpe. (Reprinted in K. Richardson and S. Sheldon (eds) *Cognitive Development to Adolescence*. Hove, Erlbaum, 1988).

Waddington, C.H. (1970). Concepts and theories of growth, development, differentiation, and morphogenesis. In C.H. Waddington (ed.) *Towards a Theoretical Biology*. Chicago, Ill., Aldine.

Wollman, W.T. (1982). Form versus content in Piagetian testing. *Science Education*, 66: 751–62.

Wood, D., Bruner, J.S. and Ross, G. (1976). The role of tutoring in problem solving. *Journal of Child Psychology and Psychiatry*, 17: 89–100.

6

Intelligence in our genes?

Most of us are aware of variability in intelligence among the people we meet and work with in the course of an average day. At a popular level the nature of that variability seems all too 'obvious' to us, even though at a more detached level we have considerable difficulty pinning it down to anything substantial. Scholars experiencing the same perception of the 'obvious', and with the practical concerns of society and its citizens to bear, have long speculated about the origins of that variability. The Ancient Greeks, including Plato and Aristotle (see Chapter 1), wrote about what was innate, and what was due to teaching. And two thousand years ago in Rome, Cicero was speaking in quite definite terms about the relative roles of nature and of fortune in determining our fates.

For various reasons, psychologists throughout the twentieth century have asked similar questions and given answers similar to those of the Ancients. The purpose of this chapter is to examine the basic concepts and the assumptions underlying the kinds of questions that have been asked about the perceived variability in intelligence; to examine the extent to which these have been *scientific* questions (as opposed to the 'popular', social questions they already are); and to examine the extent to which the answers that have been given can be considered to be scientific answers.

Two nature–nurture debates

The first issue to clarify is that there are *two*, rather than one, nature–nurture debates surrounding the subject of intelligence. The debates and arguments are quite different in terms of theoretical implication, although they are often intertwined and confused. The first nature–nurture debate is the traditional debate between 'classical rationalists' or 'nativists' on the one hand, and 'empiricists' on the other, about the origins and nature of knowledge (see Richardson 1988). Thus rationalists since the time of Ancient Greece have argued that our knowledge and reasoning is too complex and richly structured to be acquired from imperfect experience, and this structure must be 'innate' in some way. Modern exponents of this general belief are the theorists of 'modular' cognition such as Chomsky (1980) and Fodor (1983). Gardner (1984) extends this thesis specifically to the areas of intelligence, by arguing that different expressions of intelligence, such as linguistic, logico-mathematical or musical, are the distinct mental analogues of 'biological organs', each with its own genetically determined structure and processes. Thus the 'nativist' thesis is that our knowledge and reasoning is genetically *prestructured* in some important (albeit yet-to-be-described) ways. This is what is strictly implied when someone says that our intelligence is 'innate', 'genetic', 'genetically determined', and so on.

Empiricists, however, argue that knowledge and reasoning arise from experience, usually through the formation of mental associations that reflect objects and events associated in experience. Any form and structure in knowledge and reasoning is simply a reflection of these associations. This is what is meant when someone argues that intelligence comes from our experience or from the environment.

As might be appreciated, the arguments in this debate have long been about how learning and development occur: with the nativists arguing that it is really a process of maturation, assisted, of course, by a minimum amount of the right kind of experience that will 'bring out' the knowledge within; and the empiricists arguing that development is really a process of learning by formation of associations. (In fact 'constructivists', as we saw in Chapter 5, transcend this duality to some extent with still further proposals, but this has not quelled the debate – see Richardson 1988 for further discussion.) Obviously as applied to the area of intelligence, this debate is very much about the fundamental nature of intelligence, its structure, expression, and so on, in humans in general.

The second nature–nurture debate is about the source of *individual differences* in intelligence – in particular the extent to which these can be attributed to biological (genetic) rather than psychological (experiential, social or other 'environmental') factors. This debate has been much less concerned about the fundamental nature of intelligence. Like the Galtonian psychometric foundations from which it sprang, it has asserted that intelligence is some fundamental cognitive strength or power and is measured by IQ tests (or popular opinion, or personal or teachers' impressions etc.): the question is, how much of the observed *variation* can be attributed to variation in biology (genes) and how much to variation in environmental experience? Most of the nature–nurture debate in intelligence is, in fact, this particular one. It is not difficult to see why it has become so politically charged. But before going into it more closely, we need to see how the two debates have mingled.

The two debates intertwined

The clearest way to distinguish the two debates is to realise that the first is about the nature of intelligence in the general, typical member of the species. Thus the classical rationalist position would see cognitive 'organs' of intelligence as the products of evolution by natural selection, and thus present, in all important essentials, in all members of the species, although perhaps subject to some local fine-tuning from experience (in much the same way that all humans may have the language capacity and basic structure to the same extent, but vary in local expression – Chomsky 1980). Also the terms 'innate' and 'relatively innate' are used to signal the plasticity or lack of plasticity in the course of development of a character; or conversely to signal the responsiveness of that development to intervention of some sort (i.e. the immutability/changeability of development). The referent of such terms is thus the character itself.

The second debate, on the other hand, is a *population* debate. Psychologists involved in this debate presuppose that there will be genetic variation relevant to intelligence in a population of humans – the question is, to what extent does this account for the variation in 'intelligence' we see in that population?

These different epistemological roots are often overlooked, however, with many dire consequences. Common terms like 'innate' or 'environment' have different meanings according to the sense in which they are being used. Many commentators will argue that intelligence is innate, largely innate or genetically determined – terminology strictly only applicable to the first debate – when they are referring to the population debate. This collapsing of reference results in statements which are strictly meaningless. Such is Burt's (1955) famous definition of intelligence as 'innate, general, cognitive, ability'.

This imprecision and confusion is seen most acutely in the use of the term heritability. This term (usually signified as h^2) refers to the proportion of *variability* in the character (the phenotypic measure) that can be attributed to *genetic variability* rather than to environmental variability. The referent of terms like this is thus a whole population; they do not apply to any individual.

Unfortunately even experts begin to talk about heritability (a population concept) as an index of the 'relative innateness' of a *character* (e.g. Whalen 1971). Others, somewhat similarly, see heritability as the '*in*-heritability' of a character, i.e. the extent to which it is transmitted from parents to offspring in the genes. Still others see a heritability estimate for a character as an index of its immutability/plasticity in development. It is very common to hear psychologists speak of a heritability estimate as an index of the 'genetic determination' of a character like intelligence. All of these uses are wrong; this chapter aims to explain why.

Of course in some theories, informal or otherwise, there is considerable genetic prestructuring, but this prestructuring itself varies from individual to individual. Each of these may then be subjected to experiential modification or 'tuning'. In such theories we get the two nature–nurture debates completely collapsed together. Thus Gardner (1984) argues that humans have well-formed separate 'intelligences', somewhat like mental 'organs' or information-processing devices. None the less, 'While all humans exhibit the range of intelligences, individuals differ – presumably for both hereditary and environmental reasons – in their current profile of intelligences' (Gardner 1989). In such statements in particular it must be realised that two separate points about genetic causation are being made: the one concerning the 'prestructuring' of intelligence, the other concerned with individual differences in intelligence.

The immediate point is that we first need to clarify all of these terms and referents. Perhaps the best way of doing this is to examine them separately, although, as will be made clear below, the interdependence of them is critical to discussion.

The phenotype

A phenotype is an aspect of the physical manifestation of organisms, usually viewed as the 'characters' that we see varying amongst, and distinguishing, the members of a population – height, weight, eye colour, hair colour, and so on. The value of the phenotype, by virtue of natural selection, is more or less adaptive to the environment in which the species is usually found (although there are many characters which are irrelevant to adaptation). Those who wish to investigate the genetic causation of the phenotype and of differences in the phenotype obviously need to have a clear perception of the character in question. Thus the important studies in genetic variation have been done with very clearly defined, and conspicuously varying, phenotypes such as wing length, or numbers of bristles in fruit flies, or with such characters as egg-yield in chickens, and thickness of back fat in pigs. Obviously we could scarcely begin to consider the 'genetics' of any phenotype if we weren't very clear about what the phenotype is in the first place.

Strange as it may seem, this is precisely the situation with the phenotype we call intelligence. As we have seen throughout this book, there is little agreement about what the intelligence phenotype is. Indeed, not only do presuppositions vary about how best to describe it; even within the IQ tradition almost anything 'mental' seems to pass muster as a measure if it produces scores with approximately the 'right' kind of correlations with other criteria. Even the more recent information-processing theorists, adopting a more traditional scientific logic, seem content to accept a bewildering variety of measures as descriptors of the phenotype. These include things like digit span, vocabulary, analogical reasoning, verbal comprehension, deductive reasoning, general knowledge, and so on. The fact that we have no clear purchase (let alone one that permits measurement) on the phenotype, is also testified by the fact that contemporary views of the 'real' intelligence phenotype range from mental speed, through error-free transmission of nerve signals, to 'power' of metacomponents, and so on.

Within the IQ tradition, of course this problem has been avoided by adopting a pragmatic, rather than a scientific, approach with the aim of predicting educational success. Many people think that the IQ is a substantive phenotype on the grounds of this predictive quality alone. This largely explains the temptation to accept IQ as a meaningful measure of something general, tangible and persistent – i.e. a definite phenotype – even though no one knows what is responsible for the predictability. In fact even within the terms of the evidence usually accepted, this is scarcely true. As Jensen (1980) and others have pointed out, the correlations between IQ and subsequent occupational success are actually very low.

No one knows what the phenotype is, mental or otherwise, that produces the scores on IQ tests and therefore accounts for the individual differences on such scores. According to some theorists it is a fundamental biological trait. According to others, such as Sternberg (1984: 31) 'intelligence is invented. . . . It is not any one thing. . . . Rather it is a complex mixture of ingredients. . . . The invention is a societal one.' Moreover there is no evidence as to the degree to which such differences are even *mental*, at least in the cognitive sense. (Some alternatives were mentioned in Chapter 3.) As Wechsler (1974) explained:

> Intelligence behaviour . . . may also call for one or more of a host of aptitudes (factors) which . . . involve not so much skills and knowhow as drives and attitudes. . . . They include such traits as persistence, zest, impulse control and goal awareness.
>
> (Wechsler 1974: 6)

Most investigators have overcome these problems simply by pretending, as did Galton, that IQ is a quasi-physical phenotype distributed in the population, and measurable, in the same way as height, weight and physical strength. But intelligence can hardly be a physical phenotype in this sense. Even IQ test constructors have to recognise tacitly that intelligence, whatever else it is, is manifested in processes and behaviour. These don't take convenient, persistent, tangible values. Even test scores are actually impressions from numerous 'samples' of behaviour, however removed from context and social history they may be. When the latter are taken into account (see Chapters 4 and 5) the intelligence phenotype becomes even more difficult to grasp.

Even if we were to agree that IQ was a measure of a clear, objectively perceived phenotype, there is a further problem to its use for any analysis of genetic causation. This stems from the way that IQ tests are assembled as batteries of tasks. The score is simply the sum of correct responses (usually standardised to a mean of 100). Because we know and understand so little about what produces (or what prevents subjects from producing) such scores, we cannot treat them as linear measures as on a metre rule or weighing scale. Above all we cannot treat the intervals as *equivalent* – a difference between 100 and 115 say, the same as that between 65 and 80. This means that the *variability* in such scores cannot strictly be used as an unbiased description of the variability in a phenotype. The analysis of genetic causes of phenotypic variability depends on first having a reliable description of the variability in the phenotype. IQ does not give us this.

The genes

Since there is little agreement about how to describe and measure the intelligence phenotype we can hardly claim to know much about the genes that relate to intelligence. All claims to knowledge about the 'genetics of intelligence' depend on accepting a number of assumptions; even if these were valid, such knowledge would be indirect. Beyond well characterised single-gene effects which, in a tiny proportion of the population, disrupt the system entirely, we don't know anything about the genes underlying intelligence; either how many there are, of what sort, whether they vary from person to person, and if so to what extent, with what consequences and importance for development, and so on.

Nor do we know anything about how the genes for intelligence vary from person to person. They may vary considerably, as with many superficial physical characters like height or hair and skin colour; or they may hardly vary at all, as with many other 'key' organs and processes of the body. What we *do* know is that humans in general share perhaps as many as 99 per cent of their genes. Most of the claims about genetic causes of human variation in 'intelligence', in fact, come from a selective application of principles of evolutionary and population genetics, and the results of breeding experiments in agriculture, extended to intelligence. But the validity of these principles in the context of human intelligence depends on a wide range of assumptions to be discussed below.

The environment

All too often, the term 'environment', as it is used in debates about the genetic causation of intelligence and its variability, conjures up images of something akin to the manure that gardeners put around their roses. There are several problems here. The first is that, again, since we don't know how to describe the phenotype, or its development, we cannot be sure about describing the environment that is *relevant* to its development and to individual differences in that development. So we have to make guesses that are more or less plausible, depending on our presuppositions about the nature of intelligence itself.

It is not difficult to guess, in very broad terms, what some relevant environmental factors might be. A more empirical approach has been to examine environmental correlates of IQ, such as stimulation in the home, parental attitudes, rearing patterns and so on. As a result, there have been studies of different kinds of 'stimulation' and of the effects of 'enrichment', such as parental training and remedial or compensatory education, on IQ (e.g. Zigler and Trucket 1978). As Rutter (1986) concludes after reviewing such studies, although the features of the home environment conducive to optimal cognitive development cannot be specified precisely, they clearly include: parental responsiveness to children's signals; varied and positive patterns of reciprocal parent–child interaction and communication; and a range of interesting, varied and meaningful experiences and activities with both parents and other people.

(Rutter 1986: 95–6)

The way in which these correlates actually translate into a boosted intelligence is still very unclear, even if we were to have any agreement about equating 'optimal cognitive development' with IQ.

To others, the relevant 'environment' is not any static, tangible factor, but a dynamic *pattern* of social co-operation and other interactions between people. Largely for such reasons, to still others, the relevant environment differs from culture to culture (including cultures within any one society); because there is no universal intelligence, there is no measurable 'environment' detached from a specific cultural context. Whatever the case, the environment is a system of hunches that has simply not been studied systematically in relation to intelligence. So that what counts as the 'environment' relevant to the intelligence phenotype is based on assumptions rather than established facts.

As we shall see, most studies of genetic 'causes' of individual differences in intelligence do not actually measure the environment anyway: rather the environment appears only as a statistical term in a statistical model.

Genes and environment and the nature of the phenotype: the intelligence of organisms

Since Spencer and Galton, intelligence has been viewed as a 'biological' character. Recently Eysenck (e.g. 1986) defined 'Intelligence A' as 'the biological fundament of cognitive processing, genetically based (perhaps entirely so), and responsible for individual differences in intellectual competence' (1986: 1). This definition summarises the very common notion of intelligence as something 'in our genes', and yet made up of genes that vary widely among individuals, so that individual differences originate in our genes also. Similarly a wide range of theorists since Spencer have viewed intelligence as 'adaptation' to the world experienced. In this section we hope to show that the adaptation and thus the 'intelligence' of organisms can take on many forms, depending on the relations between genes, characters (the phenotype) and the state of the environment that is being adapted to.

In all characters the relations between genes and environment in the production of the phenotype (and the reciprocal relations such that phenotypes may construct their own environments) are complex indeed. Darwin's theory, which remains the corner-stone of our thinking in this domain, propounds a two-fold process: first, the production and accumulation of small variations among individuals in a species; second, the gradual build-up by natural selection (acting on such variation) of changes that would be inconceivable in a single step.

At the turn of the century, Mendel's laws of transmission of such changes from generation to generation (i.e. heredity) came to light. Later the hereditary agents themselves were identified as more or less discrete particles on the chromosomes. When the behaviour of these during cell-division and the cellular mechanisms of heredity were established, we arrived at the 'modern synthesis' of evolutionary genetics. Although that synthesis is itself being challenged (e.g. Gould 1982; Eldredge 1985) it forms the foundation of much of our thinking in this area.

Mendel (1865, rediscovered in 1900) arrived at his laws of heredity through the study of characters which were related to single genes and fell into discrete classes, such as smooth or wrinkled seeds, colour of flowers, and so on. It is now known that the expression of many characters is related to the joint action of many genes. Such *polygenetic* characters, such as leg length, head size, and so on, often show variation which is easily quantifiable, and are therefore known as quantitative or graded characters. Others, such as number of teeth or vertebrae or litter size, are expressed in phenotypic values which, although still under the influence of many genes, are all-or-none, or discontinuous, and are therefore known as 'threshold characters' (Falconer 1960). In fact, for reasons of convenience, almost all research on the genetics of populations has been done on graded characters which exhibit appreciable variation both in the genotype and in the phenotype.

Genetic variation arises from rather rare mutations (most of which are in fact lethal, and so don't survive at all) and from the way genes are re-assorted or recombined during the production of the gametes, and the fusion of gametes during conception. Thus a tremendous amount of genetic variation can be thrown up in each generation. One way or another, this genetic variation becomes translated into phenotypic variation.

Making predictions about genes and characters is relatively easy for those characters displaying 'Mendelian' inheritance. It is much more difficult for polygenic characters, simply because the phenotypes do not fall into neat categories, but are expressed as graded or as 'all-or-none' quantitative characters. Attempts to model polygenic inheritance so far have been possible only by making certain assumptions about the genes and about the environment. Kempthorne (1978), who offers a brief history of these efforts, describes the assumptions involved as 'a most remarkable defect' (1978: 17). This is none the less the kind of model that has persisted in IQ studies. The assumptions in question may be summarised as follows:

1 the genes act as collections of independent 'charges' which, as it were, are added together in any individual to determine the sum total of the 'genetypic value'

2 the 'environment' is similarly treated as a collection of 'charges' which, when added together, determine the 'environmental value'
3 these, added to the charges on the genotype, determine the 'phenotypic value'.

These assumptions, together with their idealistic consequences for the range of phenotypic values, are illustrated in Figure 6.1. It is easy to see in such a model why the 'intelligence' of the organism can be seen to reside in the particular collection of 'charges' in the genes. But there are many reasons why this model won't do. One of these is that natural selection reduces such additive variability very quickly.

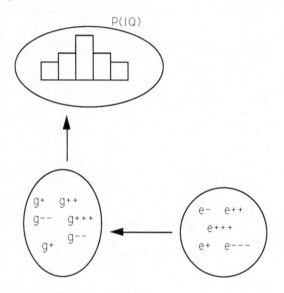

Figure 6.1 Notion of additive model of environmental and genetic charges making up the phenotype in genetic models of IQ, and producing a 'normal' distribution of phenotypic values (P(IQ)) in the population

Generally speaking for some characters, some genetic variants will have greater 'fitness' than others in that they produce phenotypes that survive better and produce more offspring that survive. By this process of selection those variants will increase in the population, and less fit variants will decrease. That is, natural selection is always tending to reduce genetic variation in characters that are important to survival. This is why members of a species are genetically so much alike with respect to such characters.

Other characters, however, do not contribute to survivability, and are thus not targets of natural selection; for these, genetic variation is 'allowed' to accumulate. This will be displayed in the heritability of the character: the proportion of the phenotypic variability that is attributable to genetic variability, usually expressed on a scale from 0 to 1. Thus, in over a hundred studies in fruit-flies, for instance, it was found that 'fitness characters' had median heritabilities of around 0.1; other morphological and physiological characters had heritabilities of around 0.35 (Roff and Mousseau 1987, cited by Barton and Tureilli 1989). This is part of the logic of natural selection. As Darwin (1959: 105), put it, 'Generally, the characters which individually vary are of slight physiological importance'. One important implication of this logic is that characters which exhibit large amounts of genetic variation are not 'fitness' characters, or have not been so for very long (Feldman and Lewontin 1975).

Even in this simple respect, the genotype is not a genetic 'bean-bag' in which genetic variance is allowed to accumulate and become randomly assorted among individual members of the population. The genotype is itself responsive to the environment acting purely as a selection agent. But there are other reasons why the simple bean-bag model is untenable as the general locus of the 'intelligence' of organisms. To understand these reasons, we have to consider some aspects of the environment itself.

Environmental change and the intelligence of organisms

Most people tend to think of the 'environment' as something stable and constant, somehow surrounding the organisms, and more or less providing for its needs, while acting as a selection agent as just described. It is true that there are some organisms existing in some environments like this. But for the vast majority of organisms the environment is constantly changing over time, or in space, as they move around, or in both time *and* space. In such circumstances, many characters evolve which cannot be thought of as stable 'fixtures' of the organisms in the way that most physical characters can.

> There are other characters of organisms and populations which are not explicable as adaptations to particular environments. . . . These and other traits may be regarded as adaptations to the pattern of the environment in space and time, to temporal variability, to environmental uncertainty. . . . Such adaptations therefore fall into the category of strategies. When our emphasis shifts to variable environments entirely new problems arise.
>
> (Levins 1968: 10)

These problems have extremely important implications for the way in which we conceive of the biological locus of intelligence.

Slow environmental change

If the environment is changing very slowly current phenotypes may lose their fitness, but genetic variability is available by the mechanisms just discussed. The corresponding phenotypic variants may now become adaptive, so long as the genetic variants are reflected more or less faithfully in the phenotypes, i.e. there is high genotype–phenotype correlation. By such means the species remains successful in 'tracking' the environmental changes (see Figure 6.2).

This is the process of change of species over long time spans known as phylogenesis. At any one time there is an optimum phenotype, and a high correlation between genotypes and phenotypes. In a very crude, and metaphoric, sense it may thus be supposed that the 'intelligence' of organisms resides in the genes. This is, in fact, the model of the genotype-phenotype-environment complex implicit in statements such as that of Eysenck (1986), quoted above, regarding 'biological' intelligence. But it is one which applies to only very restricted circumstances.

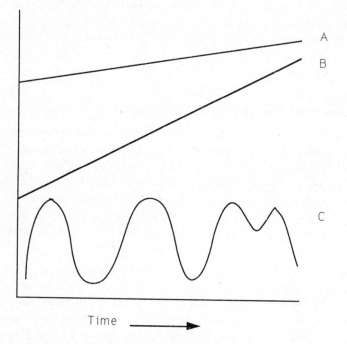

Time ⟶

Figure 6.2   Schema of kinds of environmental change and types of adaptation
Notes: A: slow, directional – adaptation by genetic selection
B: rapid, directional – adaptation by epigenetic functions
C: rapid, reversible – adaptation by epiphenetic functions
See text for further details
Source: Figure after Slobodkin and Rapoport 1974; Plotkin and Odling-Smee 1979

Rapidly changing environments

The whole process of the evolution of new species, or phylogeny, that we have just described is a very slow process. It is only successful as a response to change if the environmental changes are themselves very slow, i.e. slower than the time it takes for members of a species to produce the next generation (Plotkin and Odling-Smee 1979). Supposing changes in time and space are encountered more frequently than this? Then the environment experienced by offspring may be different from that experienced by parents. The 'intelligence' of the organism cannot be risked by translating genes directly into characters that fitted yesterday's environment but not today's. Instead, it is invested in an 'epigenetic' function which allows the development of the specific character to be responsive to the particular environment now being experienced (Figure 6.4).

There are many striking examples of the epigenetic function in organisms. Piaget (see 1980) was himself struck by the way that water snails developing close to the shore in lakes had shell forms which were different from those developing in deep water, where the water pressure, turbulence, etc., created a quite different environment. He came to use the notion of epigenesis as an analogy to describe the development of human intelligence (as we saw in Chapter 5). But there are many other examples. Some of these are obvious. Thus all organisms develop, from the same genes, an array of sharply defined tissues and organs, and not a homogenous mass of cells. This is due to the different microenvironments which the genes experience in the embryo.

Other examples have come from experimental studies with other organisms. For example the small tortoiseshell butterfly *Aglais urticae* is reddish brown with black spots when it develops in the environment it usually encounters.

> This species is abundant in Europe, including Britain, and is remarkably invariant. Yet its reddy-brown colour becomes suffused with black scales, and its black marking enlarged if it is reared in an ice-chest during late larval and pupal life. The contrary occurs, the amount of black being reduced, if the insects are forced in an incubator.
>
> (Ford 1975: 386)

Pupae of the moth *Arctia caja* emerge into insects which show little variability in their usual environments; if, however, the temperature is raised during the pupal period the resulting insects show enormous variability (see Ford 1975).

The examples of this kind of phenotypic response to environmental change during the developmental period are legion. Mayr (1963) proposed using the term 'polyphenism' to describe such characters, which he defined as 'the occurrence of several phenotypes in the population, the differences between which are not the result of genetic differences'. Lewontin (1974) and others have shown how the developmental plasticity of a phenotype can be expressed as a 'norm of reaction'. Gupta and Lewontin (1982) and Schiff and Lewontin (1986) provide natural examples of these; but the phenomenon is illustrated in Figure 6.3 with some fictitious genotypes to make the same point. Note how the phenotypic variability depends on the values and ranges of environments being experienced; and how the heritability (the ratio of genetic to phenotypic variability) will likewise vary considerably in the same population of genotypes depending on the values and ranges of environments they actually experience.

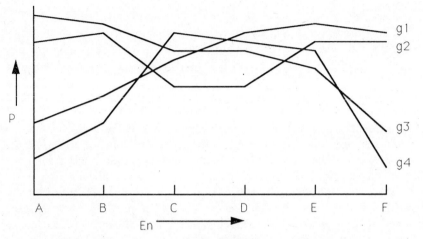

Figure 6.3   Norms of reaction of four hypothetical genotypes g1–g4
Notes: P = phenotypic values; En = environmental values. Phenotypic variability may be relatively
wide, as in the environmental ranges A to C; or relatively narrow, as in the environmental ranges
C to E. Phenotypic rank orders may change. Heritabilities may vary widely

What has happened to the genes underlying a specific character in such
changeable circumstances is that they have become organised into complex
'gene-systems', in which genes interact with each other (epistasis) in response
to the environment (epigenesis) instead of acting as separate 'charges' simply
added together. As Mayr (1970: 141) notes, 'the most important genetic
phenomena in species are species-specific epistatic systems that give species
internal cohesion'. In some cases, these interactions can be expressed as a
measurable 'norm of reaction' as we have just seen. In other such gene-systems
important 'switch' or regulatory genes can govern the expression of other,
perhaps quite variable, genes to produce an optimum, invariant phenotype.
This kind of gene-expression has been called 'canalisation' (Waddington 1957).
This phenomenon has been studied in a wide range of characters: for example
in the constant number of scutellar bristles in Drosophila, which 'is so tightly
canalised that even a considerable amount of genetic substitution will not result
in a visible change in the phenotype' (Mayr 1970: 174).

   In sum, the action of natural selection in variable, changeable environments
has produced complex epigenetic systems whose expression bears little resemblance to that of additive 'charges'. The lesson for intelligence is then clear:
in such circumstances the intelligence of organisms resides, not in the genes,
but in the reciprocal, epigenetic relations between genes and environment.

Very rapidly changing environments

This is not the end of our criticism of the 'bean-bag' genetic view of intelligence. The epigenetic view just discussed also has limitations. There is flexi-

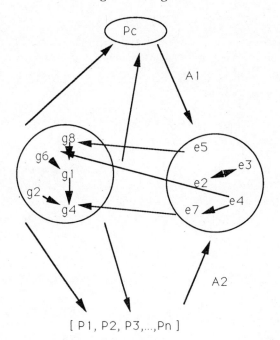

Figure 6.4 Notion of gene and gene–environment interactive systems in 'epigenetic intelligence', resulting in either a range of qualitatively different phenotypes (P1–Pn) or a canalised response in an invariant phenotype (Pc)
Note: Arrows A1 and A2 indicate that action of phenotypes affects the environment; g and e signify gene and environmental factors, some affecting the expression of others

bility of expression in the phenotype, but only during the development of the organism. Suppose that environmental change is more rapid than this (and, indeed, might even be reversed) and continues changing like this throughout the life of the organisms? In this case, neither phylogeny nor epigenesis (which covers the developmental period only) can track the changes successfully (Figure 6.2).

As we discussed in Chapter 4, these are precisely the sort of circumstances which stimulated the evolution of humans from our ape-like ancestors. Adopting a social-co-operative life-style considerably improved our ancestors' ability to cope with such changes, but added yet another layer of 'environmental' changeability in the form of highly complex human interactions. Thus was set in train an evolutionary virtuous spiral which tripled the size of the brain, and resulted in a wholly new form of intelligence.

Such changes are, in fact, those that are responsible for the adaptive intelligence we call learning (Plotkin and Odling-Smee 1979). Learning allows adaptive flexibility throughout the lifetime of the organism, and even accords to organisms the power to change and make their own environments, and to pass on that power to other individuals and to the next generation; but it does not reside in morphological or physiological characters at all. Rather it resides in the processes of social behaviour and its organisation. It certainly cannot reside in the instructions of the genes in any deterministic sense, either in fixed characters or in epigenetic processes, because, in an uncertain future environment, this would incur a severe biological penalty. Instead it must reside in the phenotype itself, either in the individual as cognitive schemas or programmes, or in the social body, or in the interaction between the two (as we saw in Chapter 4).

Here the 'end-point' of development must itself be a 'system' that can generate an infinite number of adaptive versions from a common mechanism, and do so throughout the lifetime of the organism (see Figure 6.5). The human immune system has been suggested as one analogy (Plotkin and Odling-Smee 1979); the human language system may be another (Richardson and Bynner 1984).

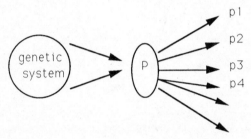

Figure 6.5 Notion of 'epiphenetic intelligence' in which the phenotype first created epigenetically (canalisation) subsequently creates 'epiphenotypes'
Note: P can be thought of as a constructor of programmes or schemas; p1, p2, etc. represent such schemas

Cognitive science – perhaps dogged by the same inappropriate models of biological causation – has been slow to take up these analogies, although Bruner (1974) has referred to 'generic coding schemes' and Holland *et al.* (1986) to 'rule-based mental models'; there have been other similar proposals (Richardson and Carthy 1989). In each of these, what must be universally transmitted in the genes are the instructions to develop a common system, that can then construct versions of the phenotype according to the particular environment, social or otherwise, actually experienced. Whatever the actual mechanism, to repeat: intelligence cannot reside in the genes, nor its variability in *genetic* variability. To do so would be to defeat the basis of its evolution: this is to *supersede* genetic variability as a system of adaptability, not to be constrained by it. This system of intelligence, at least in its culmination in humans, has resulted in adaptive success and adaptive diversity that has far outstripped that which is present in all gene-based intelligences.

We know very little, in fact, about the genetics of 'open' characters which afford life-long adaptability (Mayr 1974; Slobodkin and Rapoport 1974).

However, since we must assume that whatever system underlies it would have been subject to intense selection pressures, especially in the case of human intelligence (one indication of this is the extraordinarily rapid rate of brain expansion in human evolution – see Bilsborough 1976) then there may be little genetic variability left underlying that character. Another alternative is canalisation, a process by which diverse gene sets are brought to a common 'end-point' under the control of key regulatory genes, as mentioned above. Plotkin and Odling-Smee (1979) consider a range of such alternatives.

So neglected have such systems been as models of adaptability, that we don't even have a name for them. Richardson (1987) suggested the term 'epiphenetic' to distinguish them from, and compare them with, the epigenetic systems discussed above. But in general terms the distinctiveness of this system of intelligence of organisms has long been recognised.

> The impact of human uniqueness upon the world has been enormous because it has established a new kind of evolution to support the transmission across generations of learned knowledge and behaviour. Human uniqueness resides primarily in our brains. It is expressed in the culture built upon our intelligence and the power it gives us to manipulate the world. Human societies change by cultural evolution, not as a result of biological alteration.
>
> (Gould 1981: 324)

Summary

It seems ironic that although human intelligence is often defined as learning ability, when we consider its biological origins and genetic causation we are inclined to adopt adaptive models that are of fixed characters like height, rather than of adaptable characters of behaviour. 'The behaviour of an animal is determined by its genotype in the same way as its height is' says Rowell (1979: 4). Nothing of course could be further from the truth. Psychologists in particular should be aware of the distinctive quality of human intelligence in this respect, and should have made this more widely known. One instructive consequence of such emphasis would be the recognition of the potential for variability in human intelligence that far outstrips that conceived in the psychometrician's simple quantitiative character and list of test scores. Instead of this, the strategy of those looking for the genetic cause of differences in intelligence has been to reduce it to a model of the simple quantitative character. The likely problems associated with such a model will be identified repeatedly as we briefly consider the research that has resulted.

Investigating the genetics of variation in intelligence

As just mentioned, investigators wishing to arrive at the genetic causes of differences in intelligence have generally assumed an inappropriate level of adaptation and looked to simple quantitative models to guide them. These models are based on several assumptions (none of them facts) including the following:

1 The variability of intelligence can be treated as if arising from a simple quantitative character like height and weight, as far as its genetic causation is concerned, and this variability is accurately reflected in IQ test scores.
2 This phenotypic variability is caused by diverse genes, some 'favourable', others 'unfavourable', randomly assorted in the population.
3 These act additively, rather like sets of positive and negative 'charges' (see Figure 6.1), in the sense that the more 'favourable' genes for intelligence we have, the higher our phenotypic intelligence (IQ) will be, and vice versa.
4 The environment, too, can be treated as a constant system of 'charges' some favourable, some non-favourable, randomly distributed in the population, and similarly acting in an additive manner on the genes to produce the phenotype.

In other words, the models assume that intelligence resides in the genes, which have not been targets of selection, that mainly act additively in their expression in intelligence, in an environment of random, additive 'factors'. As we shall see, there have been many, many criticisms of the use of such models. But first let us see how they have been translated in empirical investigations.

The basic approach has been to establish models, based on the assumptions mentioned above, which predict certain patterns of data (e.g. similarities or differences in IQ scores) and then to gather IQ data from a suitable sample of people to see how the data 'fit' the models. The models, of course, depend upon separately measuring the variability in the three critical components; in the intelligence in the population (usually some form of IQ); in the environment experienced by that population; in the genotypes in the population. Since no one can pretend to measure the genotypic or genetic variance, and it would be difficult to measure the environmental variance (even if we knew what to measure, which we don't), the logic has been as follows:

1 Reason that identical twins have identical genes; non-identical twins, ordinary siblings and parent–child pairs share only half their genes (on average); and so on, down to individual members of the public, who share none of their genes for intelligence (on average).
2 Assess the similarities of IQ among these different groups and see if they match the similarities in their genes.

Identical or monozygotic (MZ) twins

We don't really know to what extent non-related humans share their genes relevant to intelligence. But we do know that identical twins, who develop from the same egg after fertilisation, share all of theirs. The question that immediately arises is whether such twins resemble each other in IQ as much as they do in their genes. But there is an obvious difficulty about this question:

MZ twins brought up together also share the same environment; the potential source of variation cannot be separated.

To surmount this problem, investigators have suggested assessing the resemblance of MZ twins reared apart. This was originally thought to be the ideal 'natural experiment' for identifying the sources of variation in intelligence. Since any covariation can only be attributed to shared genes and not to shared environments, the intra-pair correlation approximates an estimate of heritability (the proportion of phenotypic variance that is due to genetic variance). For example, Plomin and Loehlin (1989) suggest a heritability of over 70 per cent based on data summarised by Bouchard and McGue (1981).

Unfortunately this approach raises other difficulties. First, very few pairs of twins are brought up separately like this. Second, in order to separate the sources of variation, a fair assessment demands that twins have been allocated to their different environments randomly. This restriction has been rarely observed because separated twins tend to have been raised in, for example, different branches of the same family, in the same neighbourhood, and so on (Kamin 1974). There is also the constraint that ideally such pairs need to be separated at birth – indeed at conception (see e.g. Gartner and Baunack 1981)! – if confounding environmental effects are to be ruled out. This stringent condition is clearly impossible to meet.

There are other problems in the investigation of MZ twins; we shall raise these in the next section.

Comparing MZ and DZ twins

Investigators have suggested that comparing the resemblance of MZ twins with that of same-sex DZ (dizygotic or two-egg) twins could be used as a measure of heritability. Since MZ twins will share all their genes for intelligence, and DZ twins only half (on average) the difference in the intra-pair correlations (r) can be doubled to give an estimate of heritability: $h^2 = 2 \ (r(mz) - r \ (dz))$. Thus Plomin and Loehlin (1989) suggest a heritability of 0.52, again based on MZ and DZ twin correlations summarised by Bouchard and McGue (1981).

Making such comparisons involves a critical assumption, however. This is that the environment shared by MZ twins is no more similar, on average, than that shared by DZ twins. The counter-argument is that MZ twins are treated more similarly by parents, teachers and friends and are more often confused for one another; they spend more time together doing similar things, dress similarly, and even tend to study together (Rose *et al.* 1985). Again, the sources of variation appear to be hopelessly confounded.

Needless to say, there is some dispute about this (Scarr and Carter-Saltzman 1982), though attempts to investigate the 'environments' of MZ and DZ twins can hardly be described as exhaustive, confined as they have been to aspects like room-sharing, dress and so on. A major problem here (as mentioned above) is that we have little knowledge of what the environment *is* relevant to intelligence (or rather IQ). So how can we possibly know that we are randomising its effects, or not? The 'environment' relevant to subsequent performance on IQ tests may be the experience of physical stimuli emanating from physical surroundings, parents, friends, and so on; or it may be the underlying 'codes' or schemata in such experiences; or the environment may be a set of social attributions about who is or is not 'intelligent' which affect an individual's behaviour on tests indirectly, and in subtle ways.

For example, people are very critically judged on their physical appearance and other superficial attributes. One inescapable problem with twin studies is that identical twins *are* identical in appearance; DZ twins are usually quite different in appearance. This can lead to important, but usually unsuspected, consequences. Burns (1982) cites a study by Clifford (1975) who clipped passport photographs (previously rated on a scale of attractiveness) to simulated reports distributed to infant teachers. The latter were then asked to estimate the IQ of the pupils referred to. Responses indicated an appreciable 'attractiveness effect' on teachers' estimates of pupils' IQ. Langlois (1986) reviews other studies suggesting that teachers impute higher academic abilities and intelligence to the more attractive children.

Berscheid and Walster (1978) reviewed a range of similar studies indicating a strong link between physical appearance and perceived psychological attributes. Physically attractive individuals are more likely to receive positive evaluations of their competence in many spheres; they are more likely to be favoured in interviews; and to be perceived to be kinder, more sociable and more intelligent. The possibility is that such attributions by others come to be built into a self-concept which in turn influences behaviour. The review by Langlois (1986) indicates how the attribution process starts from the first moments of infancy, and continues throughout life.

> As a result of differential treatments, the developmental model endorsed here further specifies that children will learn to emit those behaviours that are consistent with the expectations, attitudes and behaviours of their parents and other socializing agents. When some children are treated *as if* they will be popular, friendly and smart and when other children are treated *as if* they will be unpopular, aggressive and not smart, these two groups of children may, then, come to fulfill their prophecies and begin to behave 'appropriately'.
>
> (Langlois 1986: 40)

Clearly even separated identical twins will be similarly subjected to such effects in a way in which other pairs of related or unrelated people are not. In fact by this process alone, identical twins would be expected to covary on any behavioural responsiveness involving a self-concept: this covariation might be expected to increase with age. These and other similar effects are clearly 'environmental'. But, because they are unsuspected, the variabilities produced by them will be counted in equations as 'genetic variance'.

This is only one illustration, in fact, of a very general problem in the use of such models, in which the environment appears as something that is 'left over' when the genetic variance has been estimated. As Wachs (1983) notes, a major problem

> with using environment as an unmeasured statistical term is that it does not meet the major criteria . . . for evaluating environmental influences. In no way can these studies be represented as using a direct measure or manipulation of the environment. Rather, what we have is a statistical term which may or may not contain environmental variance.
>
> (Wachs 1983: 400)

So much for assumptions about the environment. Additional problems arise from the 'genetic' assumptions. As already mentioned, the very nature of the method of calculating heritability from twin correlations, or other more complex methods of model fitting (e.g. Eaves *et al.* 1978; Heath *et al.* 1989) assumes that all or nearly all genetic variation is additive (see Figure 6.1), rather than non-additive or interactive (as in Figure 6.4). We have already mentioned Kempthorne's (1978) verdict on this assumption as 'a remarkable defect'. And as Barton and Turelli (1989: 342) concur, the 'additive gene action model is the basis for most quantitative genetic theory, and yet it is hard to know how often it applies'.

Many potential problems arise from this assumption. Perhaps the most serious is that the model equations are such that if this assumption is false (and, as argued above, it might well be) the environmental source of variation is considerably underestimated still further. But, as Grayson (1989: 598) notes, 'any twin data can always be accounted for without recourse to any additive genetic variance at all. . . . In fact the assumption is made that all (or as much as possible) of the genetic variance is additive'. But the consequence of this is that 'Current models for twin analysis are simply incapable of allowing genuine environmental contributions fully to express themselves' (1989: 603)

We have to add to these problems, too, the seemingly perennial one of investigators being extremely relaxed over what they call 'intelligence' and what they call an IQ test. A recent example of this problem is the report by Lynn *et al.* (1989) who administered 'the synonyms scale of the Junior Mill Hill Vocabulary Test' to school-age siblings. The results of this (part) test appear in all tables as IQ, and are referred to throughout the report as IQ or intelligence. Moreover, the authors go on – quite unabashed – to declare, 'The correlation for IQ confirms the operation of both genetic and shared family effect on intelligence' (1989: 499).

Given these problems about the use of unlikely assumptions and the lack of procedural rigour, it is perhaps not surprising that, not only is there much dispute about them, but also studies that have been done produce widely different estimates for 'heritability' (see e.g. Plomin and Loehlin 1989).

Adoption studies

Another approach has been to study the intelligence of adopted children in comparison with that of their natural and their adoptive parents.

> Adopted children on the other hand, provide almost as useful data as the rare identical twins reared apart. Adopted children are not genetically descended from the family of rearing, and therefore environmental differences between families are not confounded with genetic differences in the children if the adopted children are randomly placed by adoption agencies.
>
> (Scarr and Carter-Saltzman 1982: 833)

This approach depends on comparing the resemblances between children and their biological parents (with whom, it is reasoned, they share half their genes for intelligence, on average) with those between the same children and their adoptive parents (with whom they share none of their genes for intelligence theoretically). Again formulae exist for converting any differences in resemblance into heritability estimates.

Several such studies have been done over the last fifty years or so and these have revealed that the IQs of adopted children correlate more highly with those of their biological parents than with those of their adoptive parents. This has led to claims of substantial heritability for IQ. For example, one study suggested that the adopted child–natural parent correlation was around 0.35, while the adopted child–adoptive parent correlation was 0.1 or less (Honzik 1957). This suggests a heritability of at least 0.50. These results are taken by Scarr and Carter-Saltzman (1982) to be 'dramatic illustration of the effects of genetic resemblance on intellectual resemblance' (1983: 842). More recent results from the Texas Adoption Study have been taken to suggest heritabilities of 0.62 at age 8 years (Horn *et al.* 1979) and 0.70 at age 17 years (Horn *et al.* 1986, cited by Plomin and Loehlin 1989). Results from the Colorado Adoption Project have been taken to suggest a heritability of 0.50 at age 4 years (Plomin *et al.* 1988).

The problem with such studies, however, lies in the last clause of the statement by Scarr and Carter-Saltzman quoted above: randomness in environmental sampling is extremely difficult to achieve. Bias stems from a number of sources. For example, adoptive agencies tend to place children for adoption into families that they think are 'suitable'. Moreover, adopting parents are not themselves representative of the general population. They badly want children; they tend to be older; they tend to have better than average socio-economic security; they are carefully screened by agencies in relation to a variety of other attributes; and the·very nature of the relationship may disincline adoptive parents from trying to make these children more like themselves. In other words adoptive parents as a group present a relatively restricted range of homes and environments. This alone would make a substantial correlation between them and adopted children in performances extremely unlikely (Rose *et al.* 1984).

To be sure, some efforts have been made to 'measure' the environments of adoptive homes for purposes of establishing 'matched' family groups. In such matched groups the parent–child correlations can be checked for bias resulting from social status or other unrepresentative factors that might arise in adoptive homes (e.g. Plomin and DeFries 1983). But these matchings are based only on impressionistic ratings, made during a relatively short visit to the homes, of such things as the 'intellectual climate', the 'quality' of maternal care and interaction, and the presence or absence of certain articles. As Wachs (1983) notes, these ratings are extremely limited and probably conceal far more than they reveal. One reason they are limited is that, again, we do not know what the intelligence-relevant environment *is*, so that the question of *what* to rate is based largely on intuition. Moreover, it is difficult to know how to control for the simple fact of being adoptive parents fully knowledgeable of the fact that the child in question is not their natural child.

Another problem is that of ability attributions based on physical appearances, which we mentioned above in the context of twins. Here the problem may arise from the fact that adopted children will always tend to look more like their natural parents than their adoptive parents with all the consequential 'self-concept' effects mentioned above. Moreover, the effects would be such that any covariation between natural parents and offspring arising from this source would tend to increase with age. Yet this covariation, which is clearly 'environmental', would be treated as 'genetic' in the interpretation of correlations.

There is also the problem of adequate measures of intelligence in such studies, given that it entails testing at least two sets of adults and at least one set of children. Plomin and DeFries (1983: 278) note with respect to their adoption study that 'a decision was made at the outset to devise a test battery to sample extensively and broadly rather than intensively and narrowly'. Such decisions may be understandable in data-rich studies, but they are bound to limit the strength of conclusions. Other studies have even used 'estimates' of parents' IQ from number of years at school or even from 'interviews' (see Kamin 1974).

In view of problems like these, it is perhaps not surprising that reported correlations are widely divergent. Given this degree of methodological uncertainty it is scarcely surprising that arguments about the findings continue.

Summary

It needs to be stressed that there are very many studies of this type, of which those just mentioned are only illustrative. As stated above, the purpose of this chapter is not to give an exhaustive, blow-by-blow account of results and interpretations, but rather to raise the crucial issues. So what can we make of twin and adoption studies of this type?

Many people (e.g. Scarr and Carter-Saltzman 1982) look at tables of correlations concerning twins and adopted children and get quite excited about them. To them the data seem simply to scream 'GENES' in bold letters. This in itself is a remarkable response, especially in view of the many assumptions entailed at the outset of such studies. There are many alternative explanations for such patterns of correlations. Some of these were mentioned above; others have been mentioned elsewhere. But there are many more problems of interpretation.

First, we have to remember that we don't know what these are correlations *in*. Intelligence (whatever that is) is one explanation; but there is little agreement about what that is, so we really don't know. Equally though, the correlations could depend on attention similarities, or test-taking confidence similarities, or covariation in other non-intellectual factors involved in test-taking, including, perhaps, what Wechsler (quoted above) called 'persistence, zest, impulse control and goal awareness'. Resemblances in any of these could be the result of differential resemblances in experiences, which are impossible to rule out because we simply do not know what experiential or environmental factors are most crucial to subsequent performance on IQ tests.

This last point is important in another way: critics are constantly being challenged to find 'environmental' models that explain the data and, when they do so, of only offering 'ad hoc, environmentalist arguments' (Scarr and Carter-Saltzman 1982: 844 – who also suggest that the main interest of critics is simply to put road-blocks in the way of basically sound investigation). Such difficulties and disagreements are bound to arise when we have no purchase on what the relevant parameters and variables are.

Making the data interpretable either way involves making so many assumptions as to render conclusions virtually meaningless. The whole process becomes a kind of game such that, as Jacquard (1983: 474) put it, 'One can wonder why so much trouble is taken to measure a parameter linked to a concept which is usually not definable'. Many other authors have made the same point about the realisation of an impossible goal (e.g. Richardson and Bynner 1984; Rose *et al* 1985). Schiff and Lewontin (1986), observing that over a hundred such studies have been done in the last hundred years or so with no new information produced, ask: 'Since these studies provide essentially no genetic information, one can wonder why society has paid scientists to repeat essentially the same observation for so long' (1986: 206).

Part of the game, then, entails relaxing standards of investigation, which, in this of all fields, ought to be of the highest. Among minimum requirements are the following: the way in which the term 'heritability' or other 'genetic' terms are being used needs to be systematically defined (c.f. Jacquard 1983); whether or not the many assumptions that enter into calculations are likely to be true needs to be clearly stated; the many other parameters, such as 'intelligence' and the 'environment', that enter into the equations, need to be far more critically defined.

In their survey of the literature Schiff and Lewontin (1986) concluded as follows.

One of the most striking features of the literature and the discussions of human behavioural genetics, and especially of human intelligence, is the degree to which a supposedly 'scientific' field is permeated with basic conceptual and experimental errors. Indeed . . . much of the discussion of the biology of intelligence would simply evaporate if fundamental biological and statistical notions were applied to the genetics of human behaviour with the same degree of rigour and logic that is standard in, say, the study of milk yield in cattle or body weight in mice.

(Schiff and Lewontin 1986: 169)

The most crucial issue, however, is why we should bother to carry out such studies.

Why pursue the heritability of IQ?

Methodological problems aside, we are entitled to ask why we should pursue such investigations, anyway. To some investigators the answer is clear.

The question To what extent are existing intellectual differences among individuals due to genetic and to what extent to current environmental differences in a specific population? is scientifically important and has many possible implications for the design of environmental programmes to enhance people's lives.

(Scarr and Carter-Saltzman 1982: 815)

This point is a very common one: in spite of formidable methodological and conceptual difficulties, knowing the heritability of intelligence will help us to intervene *environmentally* to promote intelligence. Can this be true?

The answer that has been put many times by many other authors is 'No, this cannot be true'. To understand this we have to appreciate that apportionment of variance as between 'genetic' and 'environmental' sources is not an apportionment of causes (Feldman and Lewontin 1975). If it was, we would be able to predict the consequences in terms of phenotypic values (e.g. raised or lowered intelligence), either for the population or for any individual within it, of any environmental perturbation. All the twin and adoption studies, and all the estimations and model-fittings that have been done to date, have moved us no closer at all to this goal. This is because such studies (even if we could accept their results) provide only an observational 'snapshot' of current variability in a current population experiencing the current range of environments. As Figure 6.3 illustrates, a different set of environments might have produced quite a different story.

Understanding the *causes* of phenotypic variability in humans entails carrying out properly controlled experiments. Heritability estimates, or model-fitting to twin and other family data, is quite irrelevant to this task: they in no way, *and never could*, identify what manipulations or interventions would or would not be consequential and in what ways. In the case of simple quantitative or epigenetic characters, only the establishment of a 'norm of reaction', as described above, can predict the consequences of any environmental intervention. And even this involves first isolating the specific genotypes (no mean task for a character like intelligence), with manipulations and follow-up studies over several generations, while, of course, overlooking all kinds of ethical questions. But, as argued above, variation in human intelligence might not even be of this type: rather it might best be described as 'epiphenetic'. In other words the variation in a 'socio-historical' character, evolved to be constructed both individually and socially, like human language, with perhaps little if any effective genetic variability among humans, and with all kinds of biological advantages.

The dangers of false heritability attributions

Plomin and Loehlin (1989, citing Snyderman and Rothman 1987) boast that, 'A recent survey of 1020 social scientists and educators indicate that behavioural genetics has turned the corner in terms of making the case that individual differences in IQ are at least partially inherited' (Plomin and Loehlin 1989: 340). If the game is indeed one of social persuasion they need scarcely have worried. Such explanations for human differences, and especially for human failures, are a common part of the social and educational scene. Edwards and Mercer (1987: 129), for example, in a study of classroom interactions, note a widespread 'assumption on the part of teachers that educational failure in individual pupils can be attributed to individual factors, and principally to innate ability'. Many other illustrations of the social power and the social pervasiveness of the 'innate differences' hypothesis could be given.

No amount of heritability analysis can actually *support* such conclusions: but support is what is tacitly taken from them. This in turn leads to all kinds of careless thinking and talking, some of it with serious social consequences. For example, Lynn *et al.* (1989) – analysing, as we saw earlier, a set of synonyms taken from a vocabulary test – claim that twin and sibling correlations 'indicate that genetic factors play a significant role in the determination of . . . intelligence' (1989: 500). It ought now to be clear why correlations aiming to describe population parameters can tell us nothing about the determination of a character.

More serious is the notion that population parameters like heritability can indicate the causes of differences between *groups* (e.g. between different 'races') in measures like IQ, and thus imply that one 'race', say, may be genetically inferior to another 'race' in intelligence. The *scientific* pretensions of this idea, associated with the IQ-testing movement from its inception (Kamin 1974), have fortunately been decisively purged (e.g. Rose *et al.* 1984). But the popular pretensions are all too durable, as just mentioned.

The assumption that human variation is essentially *genetic* variation has pervaded all twin and other family resemblance studies, as we have just seen. But the assumption is not confined to such studies. As Schiff and Lewontin (1986) note, after a brief survey of genetics textbooks, 'The possibility that important human variation is not genetically based is simply not considered' (1986: 188). What is puzzling about this is that direct studies of the genetic variation in humans have long been revealing that humans may share as many as 99 per cent of their genes (e.g. King and Wilson 1975). This draws into perspective the methodological assumptions of, for example, twin studies, as described above. As Washburn (1978) explained, the whole calculus on which such 'genetic' assumptions are based is grossly misleading:

> A parent does not share one half of the genes with its offspring; the offspring shares one half of the genes on which the parents differ. If the parents are homozygous [i.e. are identical] for a gene, obviously all off-spring will inherit that gene. The issue then becomes: How many shared genes are there within a species such as *Homo sapiens*. . . . Individuals (considered) unrelated share, in fact, 99% of their genes.
>
> (Washburn 1978: 35)

Other studies of genetic variability in humans have confirmed this view. As Gould (1981: 323) declares, after reviewing such studies, 'biologists have re-centy affirmed – as long suspected – that the overall genetic differences among humans are astonishingly small'. None of this would be surprising to anyone who had carefully considered the unique demands of human evolution, and of human survival, by social means, and therefore of the nature of characters other than simple quantitative traits, as we tried to do above.

References

Barton, N.H. and Turelli, M. (1989). Evolutionary quantitative genetics: how little do we know? *Annual Review of Genetics*, 23: 337–70.

Berscheid, E. and Walster, E. (1978). *Interpersonal Attraction*. Reading, MA, Addison-Wesley.

Bilsborough, A. (1976). Patterns of evolution in Middle Pleistocene hominids. *Journal of Human Evolution*, 5: 423–39.

Bouchard, T.J. Jnr. and McGue, M. (1981). Familial studies of intelligence: a review. *Science*, 212: 1055–9.

Bruner, J.S. (1974). *Beyond the Information Given*. London, George Allen & Unwin.

Burns, R. (1982). *Self Concept, Development and Education*. London, Holt, Rinehart and Winston.

Burt, C. (1955). The evidence for the concept of intelligence. *British Journal of Educational Psychology*, 25: 158–77.

Chomsky, N. (1981). *Rules and Representations*. Oxford, Blackwell.

Clifford, M.M. (1975). *Physical Attractiveness and Achievement Performance*. Paper read to the Annual Conference of the American Educational Research Association, Washington DC.

Darwin, C. (1859). *The Origin of Species by means of Natural Selection*. London, Murray.

Eaves, L.J., Last, K.A., Young, P.A. and Martin, N.G. (1978). Model-fitting approaches to the analysis of human behaviour. *Heredity*, 41: 249–320.

Edwards, D. and Mercer, N. (1987). *Common Knowledge*. London, Methuen.

Eldredge, N. (1985). *Unfinished Synthesis: Biological Hierarchies and Modern Evolutionary Thought*. Oxford, Oxford University Press.

Eysenck, H.J. (1986). The theory of intelligence and the psychophysiology of cognition. In R.J. Sternberg (ed.) *Advances in the Pyschology of Human Intelligence*, Vol. 3. Hillsdale, NJ, Erlbaum.

Falconer, D.S. (1960). *Introduction to Quantitative Genetics*. Edinburgh, Oliver and Boyd.

Feldman, M.W. and Lewontin, R.C. (1975). The heritability hang-up. *Science*, 190: 1163–8.

Fodor, J. (1983). *The Modularity of Mind*. Cambridge, Mass., MIT Press.

Ford, E.B. (1975). *Ecological Genetics*. London, Chapman & Hall.

Gardner, H. (1984). *Frames of Mind: The Theory of Multiple Intelligences*. London, Heinemann.

—— (1989). Project Zero: an introduction to Arts Propel. *Journal of Art and Design Education*, 8: 167–82.

Gartner, K. and Baunack, E. (1981). Is the similarity of monozygotic twins due to genetic factors alone? *Nature*, 292: 646–7.

Gould, S.J. (1981). *The Mismeasure of Man*. New York, Norton.

Grayson, D.A. (1989). Twins reared together: minimizing shared environmental effects. *Behaviour Genetics*. 119: 593–604.

Gupta, A.P. and Lewontin, R.C. (1982). A study of reaction norms in natural populations of *Drosophila pseudoobscura*. *Evolution*, 36: 934–48.

Heath, A.C., Neale, M.C., Hewitt, J.K., Eaves, L.J. and Fulker, D.W. (1989). Testing structural equation models for twin data using LISREL. *Behaviour Genetics*, 19: 9–35.

Holland, J.H., Holyoak, K.J., Nisbett, R.E. and Thagard, P.R. (1986). *Induction: Processes of Inference, Learning and Discovery*. Cambridge, Mass., MIT Press.

Honzik, M.P. (1957). Developmental studies of parent–child resemblance in intelligence. *Child Development*, 28: 215–28.

Horn, J.M., Loehlin, J.C. and Willerman, L. (1979). Intellectual resemblances among adoptive and biological relatives: The Texan Adoption Study. *Behaviour Genetics*, 9: 177–207.

—— (1986). *The TAP Ten Years Later*. Symposium at the Sixteenth Annual Meeting of the Behaviour Genetics Association, 18 June, Honolulu, Hawaii.

Jacquard, A. (1983). Heritability: one word, three concepts. *Biometrics*, 39: 365–477.

Jensen, A.R. (1980). *Bias in Mental Testing*. London, Methuen.

Kamin, L. (1974). *The Science and Politics of IQ*. London, Wiley.

Kempthorne, O. (1978). Logical, epistemological and statistical aspects of nature–nurture data interpretation. *Biometrics*, 34: 1–23.

King, M.C. and Wilson, A.C. (1975). Evolution at two levels in humans and chimpanzees. *Science*, 188: 107–16.

Langlois, J.H. (1986). From the eye of the beholder to behavioral reality: development of social behaviours and social relations as a function of physical attractiveness. In C.P. Herman, M. Zanna and E.T. Higgins (eds) *Physical Appearance, Stigma and Social Behaviour*. Hillsdale, NJ, Erlbaum.

Levins, R. (1968). *Evolution in Changing Environments*. Princeton, NJ, Princeton University Press.

Lewontin, R.C. (1974). The analysis of variance and the analysis of causes. *American Journal of Human Genetics*, 26: 400–11.

Lynn, R., Hampson, S. and Agahi, E. (1989). Genetic and environmental mechanisms determining intelligence, neuroticism, extraversion and psychoticism: a study of Irish siblings. *British Journal of Psychology*, 80: 499–407.

Mayr, E. (1963). *Animal Species and Evolution*. Cambridge, MA., Belknap Press.

—— (1970). *Population, Species and Evolution*, Cambridge, MA, Belknap Press.

—— (1974). Behaviour Programs and evolutionary strategies. *American Scientist*, 62: 650–9.

Piaget, J. (1980). *Adaptation and Intelligence: Organic Selection and the Phenocopy*. Chicago, Ill., University of Chicago Press.

Plomin, R. and DeFries, J.C. (1983). The Colorado Adoption Project. *Child Development*, 54: 276–89.

Plomin, R. and Loehlin, J.C. (1989). Direct and indirect IQ heritability estimates: a puzzle. *Behaviour Genetics*, 19: 331–42.

Plomin, R., DeFries, J.C. and Fulker, D. (1988). *Nature and Nurture in Infancy and Early Childhood*. New York, Cambridge University Press.

Plotkin, H.C. and Odling-Smee, F.J. (1979). Learning, change and evolution: an enquiry into the teleonomy of learning. *Advances in the Study of Behaviour*, 10: 1–42.

Richardson, K. (1987). Genotype–phenotype relations in models of educational achievement. *British Journal of Educational Psychology*, 57: 1–8.

—— (1988). *Understanding Psychology*. Milton Keynes, Open University Press.

Richardson, K. and Bynner, J.M. (1984). Intelligence: past and future. *International Journal of Psychology*, 19: 499–526.

Richardson, K. and Carthy, T. (1989). Concept models and concept functions: inference from incomplete information. *Acta Psychologica*, 72: 81–102.

Roff, D.A. and Mousseau, T.A. (1987). Quantitative genetics and fitness. *Heredity*, 58: 103–18.

Rose, S., Kamin, L. and Lewontin, R.C. (1985). *Not In Our Genes*. Harmondsworth, Penguin.

Rowell, T.E. (1979). How would we know if social organisations were not adaptive? In I.O. Bernstein and E.O. Smith (eds) *Primate Ecology and Human Origins*. New York, Garland STPM Press.

Rutter, M. (1985). Family and school influences on cognitive development. In R.A. Hinde, A.N. Perret-Clermont and J. Stevenson-Hinde (eds) *Social Relations and Cognitive Development*. Oxford, Clarendon Press.

Scarr, S. and Carter-Saltzman, L. (1982). Genetics and intelligence. In R.J. Sternberg (ed.) *Handbook of Human Intelligence*. Cambridge, Cambridge University Press.

Schiff, M. and Lewontin, R. (1986). *Education and Class: The Irrelevance of IQ Genetic Studies*. Oxford, Clarendon Press.

Slobodkin, L.B. and Rapoport, A. (1974). An optimal strategy of evolution. *Quarterly Review and Biology*, 49: 181–99.

Snyderman, M. and Rothman, S. (1987). Survey of expert opinion on intelligence and aptitude testing. *American Psychologist*, 42: 137–44.

Sternberg, R.J. (1984). Toward a triarchic theory of human intelligence. *Behavioral and Brain Sciences*, 7: 269-315.

Wachs, T.D. (1983). The use and abuse of environment in behavior genetic research. *Child Development*, 54: 396–407.

Waddington, C.H. (1957). *The Strategy of the Genes*. New York, Columbia University Press.

—— (1962). *New Patterns in Genetics and Development*. New York, Columbia University Press.

Washburn, S.L. (1978). Animal behaviour and social anthropology. *Society*, September–October: 35–41.

Wechsler, D. (1974). *Manual for the Wechsler Intelligence Scale for Children*. New York, Psychological Corporation.

Whalen, R.E. (1971). The concept of instinct. In J.L. McGaugh (ed.) *Psychobiology: Behaviour from a Biological Perspective*. New York, Academic Press.

Zigler, E. and Trucket, P.K. (1978). IQ, social competence and the evaluation of early childhood intervention programmes. *American Psychologist*, 37: 789–98.

7

Epilogue: intelligence, past; intelligence, future

Intelligence, past

In Chapter 1 we mentioned the curious dualism in the scholarly contemplation of intelligence. On the one hand, it has involved the search for some 'fundamental factor' or factors which account for the differences among people often described as 'bright', 'dull', 'smart', 'stupid', etc., and usually assumed to be 'innate'. This view has, at all times, been motivated by direct social purpose: from ideology about social powers and privileges, to the legitimation of exploitation of people (including slavery); from 'racial' preservation and eugenics, to the prediction of school performance. In the twentieth century this view has reduced intelligence to a unitary 'strength' or 'power'. The whole approach reached its apotheosis in the concept and measure of IQ, which simply provides a numerical surrogate for a particular preconception and subjective impression of socially judged intelligence, mainly to do with achievement in school.

On the other hand, there has been a more detached attempt to characterise the workings of the mental or cognitive *system*, and how these workings translate themselves into the phenomena we call intelligence. The two different approaches have split psychologists into two camps, and do to this day.

Of course, many psychologists working within the IQ tradition have attempted to 'theorise' about the basis of their measure. Much of Chapter 2 was spent in illustrating such theorising. Some of this work we decided was simply reification, in that it consisted of construing, from patterns of data, an essence, power, or factor which simply confirmed a pre-conception of such a power, or which had uncertain correspondence with reality, anyway. Attempts actually to substantiate such powers or factors have been based on the somewhat capricious methods of factor analysis. The status of the factors emerging from such analyses is extremely uncertain, and even the theorists themselves warn about reading too much of substance into them. The fact that there appears to be almost as many systems of factors as there are groups of researchers looking for them indicates the fundamental problems of attempting to wring meaning out of scores from a scale that has been constructed for social purposes, not scientific ones. In fact, all scientific attempts to substantiate the presupposition of intelligence as a unitary power (or related *set* of powers) have resulted in failure, at least in the sense that they command little agreement among psychologists as a whole. An IQ score itself seems to be related to little or nothing beyond school achievement, and there have been constant warnings about the dangers of drawing causal conclusions from correlations.

In Chapter 3 we described other, more recent, attempts to pin down intelligence, using the concepts and methods of 'cognitive' or information-processing psychology. The unitary power view seems to have reached its logical, reductionist extreme in the quest for the ultimate essence of individual differences in intelligence, namely 'neurological' efficiency, speed of processing and so on. Although allegedly based on attempts to overcome the disappointments of IQ with a more scientific approach, the self-defeating method of then evaluating all measures in terms of their correlation with IQ was noted. In any case, far from revealing a psychometric philosopher's stone, each of these measures has proven to be riddled with problems of reliability and interpretation.

Other approaches within the information-processing framework, such as the componential approach, represent distinct efforts to get 'beyond IQ'. The experimental literature generated by this approach contains a wealth of interesting findings. But, again, there have been enormous problems of interpretation. Some of these problems appear to arise from the preconceptions of the nature of intelligence fundamental to the approach: sequences of independent, mechanical operations; best observed in discrete tasks; and so on. Again we noticed the seemingly self-defeating step of evaluating all results in terms of correlations with IQ: and also (in keeping with this) an enduring notion of a pervasive, universal strength or power lurking beneath all intellectal performances.

The theory of multiple intelligences also seems to be an attempt to go 'beyond IQ' by hypothesising distinct intelligence 'organs', each with its own innate information-processing routines, and so on. An account which simply throws the burden of intelligence on to innate programmes is scarcely a theory, however. We still need to have those programmes characterised by specifying components, processes, relations and so on. Physiology has brought to our attention numerous incidents of 'hard-wired' programmes, such as the breathing cycle in mammals (e.g. Wyman 1977) or the co-ordination of wing movements in the flight of insects (e.g. Huber 1980): but only by systematic discovery of the components, properties and relations in the programmes. Declaring that something is 'innate' does not remove from us the burden of specifying the intricate processes involved.

This burden must apply equally to a complex area like intelligence.

Moreover, we have to take care about the way in which the term itself is used; there is always the danger of assuming, in a preformationist sense, that 'innate' simply means 'written in the genes'. Even innate characters (and innate differences in characters) are the results of complex developmental programmes. In the context of intelligence, the term often appears to be used simply to cut theoretical corners. In fact the 'theory' of multiple intelligences appears to be more a pragmatic framework for accentuating the individual strengths that children currently have, and as a rationale for providing programmes of activity within the different intellectual domains (e.g. Gardner 1989). This is, of course, no bad thing in itself, and may be of additional empirical and theoretical value, so long as the obligatory scientific task is not obscured in the process.

The social history unfolding from the 'unitary power' idea of intelligence, and enshrined in the IQ test, has not been edifying. Although it was no part of Binet's philosophy, much of the earlier history of the promotion of IQ tests in the USA was grounded in eugenics and blatant racism (summarised by Kamin 1974). Those, like Terman (1916), who promoted testing, were immediately convinced that their test scores revealed 'vast differences . . . in original mental endowment' (1916: 4). Similarly in this country, those who followed Galton's view of intelligence did so in extension of their political views, and held strong convictions about the innate inferiority of the working class and other 'races' (MacKenzie 1979; Lowe 1980; Gould 1981). Burt (1909), although eschewing large 'racial' differences, frequently expressed his conviction about large individual differences in 'innate mental ability' among social classes in Britain, and became prominent, with other psychometrists, in the consultative commissions for the Board of Education in the 1930s.

In Chapter 1 we discussed the first expression of such ideologies in Plato's myth of the metals:

> If one of their own children has bronze or iron in its make-up, they must harden their hearts, and degrade it to the ranks of the industrial and agricultural class where it properly belongs . . . there is a prophecy that the State will be ruined when it has Guardians of silver or bronze.

There are many expressions of the same myths, the same protectionist propaganda, in modern times. While Burt (1909) was arguing that intelligence was innate, and social class differences due to heredity, Karl Pearson was insisting, in the *Encyclopaedia Britannica*, that 'It is cruel to the individual, it serves no social purpose, to drag a man of only moderate intellectual power from the hand-working to the brain-working group' (quoted by MacKenzie 1979: 137).

With the advice of psychologists like Cyril Burt the report of the consultative commission on education (Board of Education 1938: 357–8) was able to declare:

> Intellectual development during childhood appears to progress as if it were governed by a single central factor, usually known as 'general

intelligence'. . . . Our psychological witnesses assured us that it can be measured approximately by means of intelligence tests . . . it is possible at a very early age to predict with accuracy the ultimate level of a child's intellectual powers. . . . It is accordingly evident that different children . . . if justice is to be done to their varying capacities, require types of education varying in certain important respects.

(Board of Education 1938: 357–8)

In 1959 Burt was still warning:

Any recent attempt to base our educational policy for the future on the assumption that there are no . . . important differences between the average intelligence of the different social classes . . . is likely to be fraught with disastrous consequences for the welfare of the nation as a whole. . . . The facts of genetic inequality are something that we cannot escape.

(Burt 1959: 28)

More recently Scarr and Carter-Saltzman (1982), who stressed the importance of genetic studies for the 'design of environmental programmes for the enhancement of people's lives' (see Chapter 6), later in the same paper commented on the social benefits of 'diverse talents':

At an intellectual level of mild retardation, however, some individuals may make a population better adapted. It is easier to defend the idea that a population needs some people of high intelligence, who define and solve problems for the society as a whole. People of more average abilities carry out the major work of the society, but the mildly retarded, who complain less about tedium and who are willing to do jobs that few others want and to get satisfaction from them, may fulfill roles, too.

(Scarr and Carter-Saltzman 1982: 801)

In other words, there will always be menial minds to do our menial jobs!

The fact is, of course, that, from the time of Plato to the present day, the people of 'bronze', and even slaves, and others of 'mild retardation', (sometimes barely classified as human) have time and again *become* the Rulers and Guardians. On such denial of the ideology of the time the progress of civilisation has depended. The social and political presuppositions of the modern versions of the myth of the metals are, however, clear. And, as always, they become even clearer when the myth is challenged. Thus Vernon (1979: 331) links 'the current attacks on intelligence tests' with the breakdown of the State, such that, unless 'the social climate regains some of its earlier assurance and stability, I fear that we may experience a gradual breakdown of Western mores and standards'.

In spite of the lessons of history, the most prominent theorists in the psychometric tradition have been concerned to demonstrate that the differences in test score which they describe as 'intelligence' are largely 'innate' differences; i.e.

'in our genes'. Chapter 6 examined the conceptual confusions and methodological difficulties that have accompanied such efforts, including the much-abused notion of 'heritability'. What has been called the 'heritability hang-up' (Feldman and Lewontin 1975) is, in reality the 'genetic inequality hang-up', even though a heritability estimate can tell us nothing about the genetic equality or inequality of individuals in a population. In fact, quite apart from being logically impossible to assess (Richardson and Bynner 1984), heritability estimates have no scientific value in the human context; they tell us nothing about how to intervene in order to change any person's intelligence; and have no implications whatsoever for a prognosis of any individual's educational success or ability to operate fully in all the institutions of society. Above all, they have no bearing at all on the inflammatory suggestion that different 'races' are genetically unequal with respect to intelligence (Rose *et al.* 1985).

Chapters 4 and 5 considered intelligence as revealed implicitly or explicitly in the efforts to characterise general cognitive functions and their development. One of the distinctive points which came to light here was another curious dualism which has pervaded the psychometric and information-processing views of intelligence, namely the separation of processes and knowledge in the functioning of the mind. Indeed, this dualism may be every bit as fallacious as the traditional mind–body problem stemming from Descartes. Many of the studies mentioned in Chapter 4 indicate the fallaciousness of this dualism by showing how intelligence or cognition may be constituted from the contexts – particularly the social contexts – within which the mind functions. Evolutionary and cultural evidence supports this view. The difficulties this socio-historical view of intelligence presents for efforts to assess intelligence in the individual in a particular (perhaps strange) context, were considered.

Chapter 5 started by considering the paradox that psychometric methods presents in the study of development. Because the IQ movement presupposes that intelligence is something that just 'grows' – and tests are constructed accordingly – test scores can reveal very little about development as such. All they can present is a kind of spectacle of maturation, namely the unchanging relative statuses of individuals on test scores as they get older. We then considered other views on the development of intelligence which takes seriously the requirement for (a) a theory of intelligence in terms of systemic components, properties and relations, and (b) a theory of development as a process of *change* in these components, etc.

Intelligence, future

All of this leaves us with some very mixed views of intelligence. In terms of Figure 1.1 and our discussion in Chapter 1, it is clear that major efforts have been made to obtain a detached view and to construct objective, testable theories of intelligence. But such efforts are clearly tied up with the functioning of the cognitive system as a whole. Since psychology has yet to provide a key conception or principle of psychological functions (in the way that, say, the structure of the atom does for chemistry, or Darwinism does for biology), it seems clear that the finding of such a key seems a necessary prerequisite to any theoretical description of intelligence. Even Spearman (1923: 5) recognised this when he pointed out that 'No serviceable definition can possibly be found for general intelligence until the entire psychology of cognition is established'. As mentioned in Chapter 3, we are still a very long way indeed from achieving this (see also Richardson 1988). Doing so will require measurement, of course; but it will also require discipline, criticism and patience. It may well turn out to be that, at the end of the day, we have no further use for a concept of intelligence at all, a least in the scientific sense.

The psychometric approach, on the other hand, seems scarcely to have reached beyond popular conceptions of intelligence, and remains fuzzy, *ad hoc*, and flexible. Thus we find within it simultaneous attempts to reduce intelligence to a general underlying strength or power, that explains individual differences, *and yet* to give it scientific structure, form, variegation, and so on, albeit through *post hoc* analyses of test scores. This paradox has led, in turn, to continuous, unresolved argument about whether intelligence is one thing or many; whether there are group factors or separate primary factors; and so on. The underlying problem, without doubt, is the presupposition, within the whole tradition, of what we called the 'inequality hang-up'. From Plato to Galton, through Spearman, Burt, Jensen, Eysenck, and many others in the twentieth century, this hang-up has persisted and provided the foundations of the IQ testing movement. Yet it remains such a millstone around the theoretical neck, that it is scarcely surprising that the IQ movement, and all efforts connected with it, have made so little scientific headway.

One of the least edifying aspects of this hang-up is the way that it temporises with popular views and prejudices about the ladder of innate intelligence. Like many such views in the past, including the 'flat earth' or the geocentric view of the universe, their truth seems all too 'obvious', if not seductive. At a personal level, it is probably comforting to imagine that personal achievements are due to a fortuitous endowment of some unusual genes at conception. But these are not scientific views.

Such evidence as we have for the factors influencing human achievements suggest, in fact, that the promotion of the IQ view of the world may be a severe *constraint* on the promotion of achievement. It has always been difficult to demonstrate that men and women of achievement, achieved because of some measure of general intellectual superiority such as IQ or educational success. McClelland (1973) reviewed all studies carried out up to that time which had attempted (and failed) to demonstrate such a connection, and warned of the dangers of a 'mythological meritocracy' in which 'none of the measures of merit bears significant demonstrable validity with respect to any measure outside of the charmed circle' (1973: 2).

It is exceptionally difficult to tie human achievement down to an isolable cognitive attribute. Charles Darwin, for example, was far from being a good student and only scraped his degree. Of his schooldays he wrote, 'When I left the school I was for my age neither high nor low; and I believe that I was considered by all my masters and by my father as a very ordinary boy, rather below the common standard in intellect' (quoted in de Beer 1974: 12). Of the 'mental qualities and conditions on which my success has depended', he wrote:

> I have no great quickness of apprehension or wit. . . . My power to follow a long and purely abstract train of thought is very limited. . . . My memory is extensive, but lazy. . . . I have a fair share of invention and of common sense and judgement, such as every lawyer or doctor must have, but not I believe in any higher degree.
>
> (de Beer 1974: 84–5)

Similarly Einstein was scarcely the epitome of the gifted student. He was thought lazy by his professors, who blocked his chances of university employment, condemning him to the famous patents office. Einstein was always ready to point out that Relativity had been discussed by others long before he crystallised the idea in his famous thesis, and insisted that the work of the individual is so bound up with that of scientific contemporaries that it appears almost as an impersonal product of the generation (Bergia 1979; Einstein 1982).

Many empirical studies have failed to pin down the cognitive peculiarities of high achievers. In one study, for example, MacKinnon and his colleagues compared a group of exceptionally creative architects with two other, more ordinary, groups. The individuals were asked to rate each other according to the following attributes:

> 'Grasps other people's ideas quickly.'
> 'Is flexible and adaptable in his thinking.'
> 'Has an active, efficient, well-organised mind.'
> 'Is intellectually gifted.'
> 'Has an exceptionally good memory.'

As Blum (1978) describes the results, 'All these descriptions either failed to differentiate among groups, or applied more to the uncreative ones. Similarly, scores on the Wechsler Adult Intelligence Scale showed no differences between groups'.

The only consistent factor emerging in such studies is that achievers have the opportunity, conditions and motivation for simple hard work. As Ann Roe (1952) concluded in her in-depth studies of eminent American scientists:

> The one thing that all of these scientists have in common is their driving absorption in their work. They have worked long hours for many years, frequently with no vacations to speak of, because they would rather be doing their work than anything else.
>
> (Roe 1952: 24)

The danger is, then, that the overwhelming presupposition of a ladder of innate intelligence may have the direct or indirect effect of actually suppressing human achievement. Of course, no one can 'prove' the equality of humans any more than we can 'prove' the inequality of humans, with respect to intelligence. Even if we could somehow 'see' the genes responsible for intelligence this would be no indication of how they act (with the exception that is of rare deleterious genes that are well characterised by virtue of their devastating effects on the system). Tracking such action (as we indicated in Chapter 6) would involve isolating genotypes and carrying out breeding and treatment manipulations over several generations. Even if such a bizarre experiment were remotely possible no one knows how long it would take: perhaps four hundred years would be a conservative estimate! It would be even more bizarre when we know of the possibility that humans share nearly all of their genes, anyway. The sheer impossibility of scientifically answering the kinds of questions which the IQ movement throw up ought to be apparent to anyone who gives them a moment's serious thought. Indeed they transport us to the realms of fantasy.

The only possible alternative to impossible genetic experiments, as Kempthorne (1978) points out, is to carry out 'environmental' intervention studies: 'one experiment [of this kind] . . . is better than all the data analyses of Burt, Jensen and others' (1978: 20). This is the case whether the causes of human differences are genetic or not. My extreme myopia may be 'caused' by specific genes – or it may not be. The 'treatment' is exactly the same, either way, and makes me equal with other humans in this respect. Whatever the cause, this treatment has not been arrived at by asking questions about, or doing experiments in, the 'genetics' of vision at all, but by 'environmental' experiments. When we further consider the improbability (discussed in Chapter 6) of intelligence being 'in our genes' in this very simple sense, the necessary direction of future research effort seems all the more clear.

But a move to this more scientifically positive, rather than ideologically negative, view of human intelligence requires the adoption of a presupposition opposite to that mentioned above: a presupposition of the potential *equality* of the vast majority of humans, rather than hasty negative characterisations. Indeed the development of our democratic institutions would seem to demand such a presupposition.

This leaves the question of the role of IQ tests in everyday, practical issues which face psychologists. It is important to consider this question because such tests are being constructed, sold and used by more people more frequently than ever. Even some critics of the concept of intelligence as used in IQ believe the IQ test has a useful role in predicting future achievement (e.g. Howe 1988). Achievement, here, of course, refers to the narrow sense of *school* achievement. Neither IQ nor school achievement seems to bear any relation to future occupational success. The important point to remember here is that an IQ score is simply a numerical surrogate for impressionistic ratings like those of school teachers. The danger is, of course, that people may take this to mean that the test is somehow *adding* predictability to subjective impressions, thus bolstering further the mystique of the test.

This then leads to the much greater danger, that of reifying the 'intelligence' of the test constructors as something real, and isolable, and separately causative of school achievement. Psychologists fall into this trap all the time. It is difficult not to open a psychology journal or magazine without authors referring to IQ as 'level of general cognitive functioning', or some such euphemism. Howe (1988) has shown how mistaken it is to use IQ as explanation in this sense. Given these dangers, and the fact that IQ only provides a convenient reflection of information (like teachers' impressions) abundantly available, anyway, we perhaps need to take seriously Goodnow's (1986: 88) suggestion of 'a moratorium until we know more clearly what we are trying to predict, and what the costs and benefits are of various ways of proceeding?'

The biggest danger of all lies in the combination of such reification with the Platonic myth of genetic inequality. When this combined abstraction permeates our institutions serious damage is done to large groups of individuals, and therefore to society as a whole. In the education system, for example, where the belief in 'innate general intelligence' seems to be endemic, large numbers (perhaps even a substantial majority) of young people annually leave school seriously believing that they have no 'brains' and that they are incapable of learning anything very serious. When such people subsequently become excluded from their democratically rightful roles and places in the institutions, democracy itself suffers. To minimise, or even deny, the mental resources of the vast majority of human beings, does not seem an intelligent way for us to conduct the affairs of society.

References

Bergia, S. (1979). Einstein and the birth of special relativity. In A.P. French (ed.). *Einstein: a Centenary Volume.* London, Heinemann.

Blum, J.M. (1978). *Pseudoscience and Mental Ability.* New York, Monthly Review Press.

Board of Education (1938). *Report of the Consultative Committee on Secondary Education with Specific Reference to Grammar Schools and Technical High Schools.* London, HMSO (Spens Report).

Burt, C. (1959). Class differences in intelligence. *British Journal of Statistical Psychology,* 12: 15–33.

Burt, C.L. (1909). Experimental tests of general intelligence. *British Journal of Psychology,* 3: 94–177.

de Beer, G. (1974). *Charles Darwin; Thomas Henry Huxley; Autobiographies.* Oxford, Oxford University Press.

Einstein, A.E. (1982). *Ideas and Opinions* (compiled and edited by C. Seelig). New York, Crown Publications.

Feldman, M.W. and Lewontin, R.C. (1975). The heritability hang-up. *Science,* 190: 1,163–8.

Gardner, H. (1989). Project Zero: an introduction to Arts Propel. *Journal of Art and Design Education*, 8: 167–82.

Gould, S.J. (1981). *The Mismeasure of Man*. New York, Norton.

Howe, M. (1988). Intelligence as an explanation. *British Journal of Psychology*, 79: 349–60.

Huber, F. (1980). Principles of motor coordination in cyclically recurring behaviour in insects. In P.N.R. Usherwood and D.R. Newth (eds) *'Simple' Nervous Systems*. London, Edward Arnold.

Kamin, L.J. (1974). *The Science and Politics of IQ*. New York, Wiley.

Kempthorne, O. (1978). Logical, epistemological and statistical aspects of nature–nurture data interpretation. *Biometrics*, 34: 1–23.

Lowe, R. (1980). Eugenics and education: a note on the origins of the intelligence testing movement in England. *Educational Studies*, 6: 1–8.

McClelland, D.C. (1973). Testing for competence rather than for 'intelligence'. *American Psychologist*, 28: 1–14.

MacKenzie, D. (1979). Karl Pearson and the professional middle class. *Annals of Science*, 36: 125–43.

Plato, *Republic*, Book III.

Richardson, K. (1988). *Understanding Psychology*. Milton Keynes, Open University Press.

Richardson, K. and Bynner, J.M. (1984). Intelligence: past and future. In P. Fry (ed.) *Changing Conceptions of Intelligence and Intellectual Functioning: Current Theory and Research*. Amsterdam, North-Holland.

Roe, A. (1952). A psychologist examines sixty-four eminent scientists. *Scientific American*, 187: 21–5.

Rose, S., Kamin, L.J. and Lewontin, R.S. (1985). *Not in Our Genes*. Harmondsworth, Penguin.

Scarr, S. and Carter-Saltzman, L. (1982). Genetics and intelligence. In R.J. Sternberg (ed.) *Handbook of Human Intelligence*. Cambridge, Cambridge University Press.

Spearman, C.E. (1923). *The Nature of 'Intelligence' and the Principles of Cognition*. London, Macmillan.

Terman, L.M. (1916). *The Measurement of Intelligence*. Boston, Mass., Houghton Mifflin.

Vernon, P.E. (1979). *Intelligence: Heredity and Environment*. San Francisco, Freeman.

Wyman, R.J. (1977). Neural generation of the breathing cycle. *Annual Review of Physiology*, 39: 417–48.

Index